Changing Lanes

JAMES SHERRY

authorHOUSE®

AuthorHouse™ UK
1663 Liberty Drive
Bloomington, IN 47403 USA
www.authorhouse.co.uk
Phone: 0800.197.4150

© *2016 James Sherry. All rights reserved.*

No part of this book may be reproduced, stored in a retrieval system, or transmitted by any means without the written permission of the author.

Published by AuthorHouse 07/7/2016

ISBN: 978-1-5246-3590-9 (sc)
ISBN: 978-1-5246-3589-3 (hc)
ISBN: 978-1-5246-3591-6 (e)

Print information available on the last page.

Any people depicted in stock imagery provided by Thinkstock are models, and such images are being used for illustrative purposes only.
Certain stock imagery © *Thinkstock.*

This book is printed on acid-free paper.

Because of the dynamic nature of the Internet, any web addresses or links contained in this book may have changed since publication and may no longer be valid. The views expressed in this work are solely those of the author and do not necessarily reflect the views of the publisher, and the publisher hereby disclaims any responsibility for them.

PREFACE

This is not a book of fiction or fantasy, it is a true record of my own experiences, feelings and thoughts, throughout my life, there are no figures of the imagination in this book, just real life people who were part of the everyday life. Thousands of others who grew up in Ireland during the war and in the fifties and sixties could write similar memoirs, but rarely (with the exception of a few) has anyone ever put pen to paper. After a lot of thought I decided I would do so before it was too late, for ours will soon be a diminishing generation. We are getting older. Our way of life is all but gone, and before I go, I think it is only right that some of us should sit down and put together the inside story of our experiences as a kind of document to those who can also try and explain the meaning of some of the words that people used in everyday life. What I aim to do in this book is to combine my own experience of what happened in my life and some of the people around me, together with how people lived, such as the implements they used to work their land.

CHAPTER 1

FIRST MEMORY

My first memory is a combination of many things and it's difficult to say what comes first. It seemed to me at the time like one long day or one long night- just a lot of things happening that I could not understand

I must say first that unlike the other members of my family, I was sent to my uncle Johns and his wife Alice and their family at the early age of six months because my mother had been very ill. I suppose it was only meant to be for a short while but I have not got enough information on those early days to know all the reasons, but what I do know is that I stayed there until I was 8 years and 3 months old and I was very, very happy there. They were all very loveable and wonderful people and they thought the world of me. They did not have a lot of money but they shared all that they had and they gave me the far most important thing of all –their love!

I always looked on them as my brothers and sisters and believed that was what they were, until a short time before going home. They were all adults, except Bridget who was still at school, it was her who took me to school and I can just about remember her sister Maggie who was also at school. There were eight members of this family that I lived with – two boys and six girls. Their names were John, Peter, Cassie, Alice, Annie, Mary, Maggie and Bridget.

John was brought up with Aunt Annie and her husband James Cush in Aughnacloy and Cassie and Alice lived most of their early years with Uncle Patrick and Aunt Maggie in Dromore.

They were all wonderful loving people but Peter was always special. He was everything to me, brother, father and uncle all rolled into one.

Maybe it seemed unfair to my own family to describe them like that, but that was how I felt, there were very happy years I spent there.

During the early years Peter had to leave home to find work. The first person I can remember him working for, was a man called George McMeel. He was known to most people as "Big George", he lived only a short distance away and Peter would come home a lot, but he always stayed in his place of work at night,

One of the first men outside the family I can remember was a man called Jamie Mullen he looked like someone out of a Dickens novel, he wore some kind of cloak or cape around him and an old pointed hat, his hands were black his face was black his clothes were black. He lived by himself not far from my home at that time, two other boys and myself liked to go to his house quite often. He had some very strange habits, one of these habits was that, he would take the sticks off the fire then push them to one side and when they were cold he would stand them against the "back stone" rake them with his fingers, and eat them. The two with me would be Mick "the Yankee" Treanor and Felix Treanor, better known as "Fay", although they were not related. We would tell the story about Mullen eating the cinders, but nobody seemed to believe us! There would be a few other men, "caeidhlers", who would come into our house on different nights of the week, debating all kinds of subjects and some heated arguments about politics would arise, we also heard lots of ghost stories.

Different nights of the week there might be a change of faces, there was another man "John Pat John", his proper name was John McMeel, then there was Charlie "Roadie", proper name McKenna, Paddy "Tireran" McKenna and big Mick Keenan, but Mick was young compared to the others. They were all great characters, some of these people could not read or write, but at the same time they were quite clever, I often think about what they might have been like if they had an education. Paddy Tireran could sing songs with maybe twenty verses, and even at an early age I learned parts of some of his songs and thank God for him. Paddy would always leave earlier than the rest of the other people, he used to say he had to go home to help his wife Biddy off with "the big pot", at that time if you were lucky enough to have a decent crop of potatoes, a large pot full of potatoes would be put on the fire, (on a crane-crook), this would be boiled for the pigs and the hens.

A few houses would have a crane-crook, it was made from strong iron, and the upright part of the crook was fixed to the inside of the fire place. This upright was about an inch and a half by inch and a half square, it was rounded at the top and bottom, the top was entered into an eye bolt which was fixed to the wall, the bottom end was fixed into a shallow round hole in the floor, the horizontal part was welded to the upright bar near the top, another bar was fixed from the vertical to the horizontal bar in a forty five degree angle, this was to support the weight of whatever had to be carried on the crook. There would be two or three different implements, the ends of each one would be bent in a u shaped form, which enabled them to fit neatly over the horizontal bar. These implements were all different lengths, there would be a row of holes in each one, each hole about one inch apart, the bottom of each of these would bend out ninety degrees each with a hole in the bent section, which enabled another implement to be passed through these holes, there would be two or three of these implements, they were made from a round iron bar about three quarter inch thick, the top of each one was bent about ninety degrees, about one and a half inches long, with the end slightly pointed, this could be entered into any of the holes which enabled whatever was being put on the fire to be raised or lowered to whatever height it required, so altering the amount of heat applied to the food being cooked. Whilst this arrangement was reasonably common, most homes had a bar across the inglenook which allowed you to hang the cooking pots on them.

In those times most of the houses were thatched, the thatch would come from straw which would be threshed to remove the oats or corn from it. The implement used to thresh the corn with was called a flail. This was made usually from sally and holly timber. The staff which you held in your hand was made from sally [timber], there was a hole drilled in the top of the staff, the other part of the flail was called the supple, it was slightly shorter and not quite as thick as the staff, and which had a piece of leather fixed on to the end of it. This was bound round the supple by a cord which was called a hemp, it was the same cord as the shoe maker used for sewing the shoes. The piece of flax was passed through the eye of the supple, then through the hole in the staff, this was called a middle.

Everything had to be of good quality as it took a pounding, when you swung the flail, the supple struck the corn, and you had to let the staff roll round in your hands, if you held it tight something had to give, either the middle or the leather fixing, because either one of them could become too taut and break.

In these times most farmers had only a few acres of land, so they would bring their corn into the barn to thresh it, which is where the preparation of the straw for thatching took place. There would be a wooden platform put on the floor and the corn was threshed on this, it was all quite skilful work, the straw had to be kept nice and tidy, they would thresh for maybe a half hour, then they would "draw" the straw. They used a piece of wood with some nails driven through it, it was used like a comb, pulled through the straw to remove any bits of grass or rubbish.

I believe living with John and Alice for the first eight years of my life gave me a lot of character. They were a real father and mother to me and I called them Ma and Da. Alice would go to the market in Aughnacloy on a Wednesday and she would always bring sweets home. She would put some away so there would always be sweets in the house. She was so kind.

Then one terrible day, tragedy struck our little home, Alice the woman I thought was my mother had a stroke! It was something I can never forget, I was alone with her when it happened, and it had just turned dark. She had made some bread that day and she was going to get me some bread and jam, I was about 6 years old. As she went to a cupboard that was near the door, she turned and looked around at me. I thought she was crying, but then she fell beside the door. I thought she had just fallen over and hurt herself and would be all right in a little while! When she did not get up, I was scared out of my wits, I screamed and cried until I could cry no more. A young girl called May Treanor was not far away, she heard me and came along, and ran down to where my Uncle John and his daughter Annie were working at the corn. It seemed a long time before they arrived. Alice was a big heavy woman and I was trying to lift her. Before long there seemed to be quite a few people around, as there were no phones anywhere around at that time, someone had to go into Emyvale for the Doctor, cars were few and far between, so it had to be on the bike. Anyway the Doctor arrived some time later, I can remember him saying that she would be in bed for a long time, but sadly she never fully recovered. After sometime she was able to sit in an armchair by the fireside. Sometimes she would seem quite well and then at other times it would be hard to understand her.

I remember when first I started school she seemed quite well and seemed to know what was going on. I went into her room to talk to her before I went off to school and she seemed very happy, I can't say how long after that it was before she died, as everything seemed a long time at that period of my life. When she died everyone was trying to make it easy for me by telling me I would meet her again in a lovely place called heaven.

A great amount of people came to the house for the "wake" and there were not enough seats for all of them, so they had to be borrowed from neighbours, this was my first experience of a wake, and wakes were big occasions in Ireland, and still are in and around our townlands to the present day. Later on in the night, Peter took me to a quite spot to talk to me, he said he was going to take me to Big Georges, where I could stay the night, and have a good night's sleep. I didn't have any problem with this at all, I knew who big George was, I was often in his house before, and his wife was a very kind and lovely woman. Peter stayed with me until I fell asleep, and then he came back around in the morning and took me back home again. This went on for a few days until things got back to normal, or maybe it wasn't normal. It took me a long time to get over the fact that she was no longer there, and I was only a child, so what must it have been like for the rest of the family! Poor Annie and her dad must have had a really hard time. Alice was a big heavy woman and would have to be lifted in and out of bed, there were no hoists or mobile wheel chairs, and there were no baths or inside toilets. It was hard work for poor Annie and her dad, and never any grumbles from either of them. Annie took over the task of looking after us, and getting Bridget and myself off to school.

Tragedy was to follow our wee home, when about fifteen months later, Annie died…. she was only in her twenties. Up until then these were the only family I knew.

STARTING SCHOOL

I NOW COME to where I went to school, that was in Carrickroe [old] School. This was in the time before Alice, who I regarded as my mum, and Annie died.

The schoolmaster was Mr McEntee, and the teacher for the infants and other lower classes was Miss Coyle. I never got as far as Mr McEntees class as I had to change schools before I reached his class. I remember well the first day I went to school, Alice was alive then, and I went to her room to see her before I went off to school. She seemed to know what was going on, and was happy to see me starting school.

Bridget took me to school, the infants (which I was one off), would be allowed out at 2 pm, but could wait for the bigger ones if they wished. After a while at school I got braver, sometimes I would go early, along with Fay Treanor who lived just across the field from me. He had a habit of getting into mischief, he loved to throw stones on the tin roofs, and many of the animal sheds were roofed with corrugated iron sheets, as they remain today, and scare the animals inside. I suppose he did not mean any harm in it, it was just a bit of fun to him. He was a great shot with a stone, I remember him throwing a stone down Mr McCafferys chimney one day, Mr McCaffery ran the post office, and we just stood there in disbelief as the stone flew down the chimney pot, until Mr McCaffery came out shouting, I had not done anything, but I ran off along with Fay, that's what it would be like most times, but it had its good points as well. All the boys around his age were afraid of him, but I always felt safe in his company.

After school hours my playing chum was a boy called Mick Treanor, his family were known as the "Yankee Treanors", I think because his father and mother were in the U.S.A. for a number of years, so Mick would be called Mick the Yankee. It wasn't that I was a fair weather friend to my school chum Fay Treanor, but he would not have as much spare time, for his father found lots of jobs for him to do after school, not dissimilar to another that I would meet, but I digress. Mick and I got on well together we had the odd row, but we would be friends again in no time, he lived just a few minutes away from me, but went to a different school. He went to Bragan school. He was a good kind boy, he would bite a sweet in half and share it with you, we spent a lot of time in both our houses, and he used to sing a lot of comedy songs, he was a very good singer.

The house would be full of people some nights, and he could get up and sing in front of them all, I was too shy to do that, I would sing in my own house, or out in the fields. A lot of the people that time would sing through their noses, and I used to copy them. Bridget would say "don't sing through your nose sing the right way".

Some years later, when I would hear the country and western singers on the old 78 records on the gramophone, I thought maybe I was before my time, my favourites were Jimmy Rogers and Hank Williams, and I suppose it seemed strange for a youngster to have that taste in music.

The first musical instrument I ever remember hearing was a melodeon, a man called Owen Hughes had one and played it very well, he lived just as short distance away across the field. When he would play I would go outside and listen, I thought it sounded heavenly, but I was not happy until I saw him play it inside his own house, when I could sit beside and watch him, I thought he was magic.

My next encounter with music was bagpipes. It was on a Sunday evening. I was outside playing about, I could hear this lovely music in the distance, sometimes it seem to be getting close, and then it would nearly fade away, I suppose as it reached the top of the hills it got louder and down in the hollow it faded, but at last this big man came into view with the pipes over his shoulder. At the time I did not know what they were called, but when I got back into the house they told me what they were, but getting back to the man who was playing the pipes, he was a giant of a man, he must have been six foot six or more, I had never seen or heard anything like this before, it was some sight for the eyes of a child in those days. I was completely charmed by his music, he was called big Pat "Oiney", that was just a nickname, I think McKenna was his proper name, I followed him all the way around the road to Drumbristan cross, it was like the pied piper, I think I was in another world for a while, but it was getting dark and with all the ghost stories I had heard, there was a ghost at every lane and gate along the way, I ran all the way home and arrived safely to tell of what I seen and heard!

CHAPTER 3

GETTING READY FOR HOME

THESE WONDERFUL PEOPLE who reared me with such loving kindness were trying their utmost to make it easy for me. The big attraction was Peter, (the man I thought was my brother), who up until a short time before I went home, was working for a man called Tom Brush. The Brush farm was quite near to my family home where I was going to live, and I would be able to see Peter quite often. I would have lots of brothers and sisters to play with. They were painting a rosy picture, but even the best planned events have pitfalls and all sorts of problems. Things adults, never mind a child, could not foresee.

I had a long way to go to be part of the family, it was not anyone's fault, there were ten of us in the family at this time, Maggie, Cassie, Peter, Nelly, Felix, Florence and Agnes living at home, the youngest had not yet been born when I arrived. Patrick lived with our uncle Patrick just a few minutes walking distance away, and John, as I mentioned before, lived with our grandmother. The only member of my own family, that I knew a bit better than the rest was my brother Patrick, but up until arriving home to Dromore, he was always known as Packie or Packie Joe. Sometimes he would come to Knockabeny, which was the name of the town land where I used to live. He would come during his school holidays, he would help with

– 10 –

the hay and with the turf in the bog, we would have great fun, and it gave me more confidence as well, I would let the local boys know that I had a big brother around, it made them give me more respect, in other words, if they did anything to me, he would get them, and no better man to do it.

The next day after arriving home, it was not long before Felix and I got playing together, he had a little gun which made a little cracking noise when you pulled the trigger, and I had a gun as well. It was a bit bigger than the one Felix had, and it fired caps which made quite a good bang. I would let Felix have a go on it as well. One day when our dad had been trimming some hedges and Felix was going with him. Felix asked me if I wanted go along with them too but, my sister Nellie spoke, and told me that I was not allowed to go, I didn't ask why, or say anything more about it, but I learned over the years that Nellie could be a bit bossy!

My brother Peter used to go out to set "dulls" to catch rabbits, I suppose the proper word for dulls would be snares, he was a dab hand at it. He would set the dulls after school, and then go round them in the morning to see if he caught anything, He used to call it "looking my dulls", even at that age he knew how to make a few shillings.

He was always a bit of a rascal for getting you into trouble, he would go jumping across ditches, that he could hardly manage, and then tell you to do the same. He would say to, "go back and take a good run at it", when you couldn't jump it, you would have to go looking for an easier place, he would be gone out of sight and I would be out of my mind, because at that moment I would not have a clue where I was, then he would turn up with a big smile on his face. He would always be up to some mischief, and he never changed throughout his adult life, He was lucky to get away with some of the things he did!

My mother's cousin lived in Glasgow she was called Nellie Treanor, she was very kind, she would send toys and sweets over to us at Christmas. Everyone's names would be on whatever they were getting, but of course she was not to know that I had arrived home, I remember Mum and Dad explaining and saying that they would get me something the next day in Aughnacloy, and they did, and my other family hung my stocking up for me as well, and they had some nice things for me, so everything worked out alright after all. Before I left my other family, I said Santa Claus will not know where I am, and they said "don't worry we will hang up a stocking for you", and sure enough a few days after Christmas they brought me down some nice things that Santa brought me for Christmas, there must have been something worked out between both families, because one of the things Felix got was a little horse, and one of the things I got was also a little horse. In those days most of the farmers had small farms and could not afford to keep two horses so what they did was join plough. This was when two farmers who knew each other and got on well together, pooled their resources and make a team of two horses, and then they would agree who would get the first turn, and then shall we say, plough one field "time about", or whatever method was agreed to.

The land in our part of the Country was also very hilly, which meant that, one horse alone would be unable to plough uphill, and it would take ages doing one "score", a score was only nine inches wide, so that walking up the hill idle (not ploughing), was a waste of time, two horses pulling could plough uphill, and that was what the joint plough was all about.

At last the time had come to leave and be taken from a good home to the home I had only heard about. I was excited and afraid at the same time I suppose, because I would be near Peter but I would be going to a new family and a new school. I was worried that I had no protection in the person of Fay Treanor at the new school!

I can remember the evening well that I left for my new home in Dromore, it was the first Sunday in November, I was eight years and four months old, we always had a holy hour in Carrickroe on the first Sunday of the month, this must have been close to Halloween as we always called it. At this time Cassie had taken over the running of the house, after Annie died, doing the cooking, and looking after all the members of the family. Cassie was a great cook she could make up her own dishes and make all sorts of nice things. She was real special at apple pies, she made some lovely cakes and pies for Halloween, she said would make something nice for my Mum and Dad, these were my real Mum and Dad, they were coming to take me to my new home in Dromore. I don't think it sunk in until they arrived, and Cassie started putting my belongings together, Maggie and Bridget were in tears, they were the youngest of the family. These were unforgettable moments, this was the place where I said my first words, took my first steps, made my first communion, it should never have been allowed to happen like that.

My good friend Mick Treanor came over to say good bye, he did not come into the house, he was sad, and so was I, we had a lot of fun together, I was comforted by the fact that I lots of brothers and sisters to play with.

When everything was ready, I set off for my new home with my Mum and Dad, Cassie Maggie and Bridget walked out the road with us as far as James "Tammy" McKenna's. There were plenty of tears, they all kissed me good bye, I can remember their salted tears on my face, things would never be the same again for any of us, it did not mean that I did not love them as much, that never changed, and I know their love for me never changed, but we were parted, and I don't think I understood what was happening, or how things would change!

We walked for what seemed like ages, I remember being on this part of this road before, I had been taken down as far as my grandmothers, my mother's mum house, it was probably a trial run! We stopped there again, and it was there that I first met my brother John, who lived with our grandmother, uncle James, aunt Roseanne and another man called Frank Wallace was there as well. He was also brought up by my grandmother. Finally we reached Dromore, and home, it was a big encounter for me. There seemed to be an awful lot of people in one small house, most of them I had never seen before, they all had little stools which our dad had made for them. He told me that he would make one for me as soon as he got time, but in the meantime, I would have to share with the others. Anyway, the stool never got made, as my dad's health began to fail, shortly after I got home. Sometimes we would push two stools together for three of us to share, but this arrangement did not always work very well, I was the intruder. There was resentment from the other children, and on all too frequent occasions, the two stools would move apart and we all know the result of that... and the cause....PETER

The one good thing about the move was I did not have to go to school for a week or two, but I did not like it very much when I had to face up to it, there was quite a lot of hostility, it was not like starting as an infant again, I was an outsider and would have to be tested out! The bigger boys were arranging other boys to fight me, nobody likes being called a coward, so you fought, even though you did not want to, and the better you done, the bigger the boy would be the next time, and you did not like going home with cuts and bruises. I hated everything about it, and I had two older brothers still at school, but they were a good few years older, and had their own games to play, and were not too bothered about us younger ones. I suppose I was expected to fight my own battles. After some time I just had to come to terms, or adjust to the situation as best I could,

Getting back to Christmas and the presents, never mind Christmas or the presents, what I was getting worried about, was that Peter had not been round to see me since I came home about two weeks ago, which seemed a long time to me, but when he did, it was the best present of all, looking back at it later on, he had to tread carefully, and not come round too often, in case I got upset, so it was not like I thought it would be. I thought I would see him more often I suppose everyone concerned knew best how to handle it. After some time I was allowed to go round on some Saturdays to the place where Peter worked, this was great fun when he would be ploughing, he had a sack with some hay in it, he would put this on the plough and set me on it, and ride up and down as long as I liked. The people he worked for were very kind, I had lots and lots of lovely food, they would give me the same size dinner as any of their work men and I could eat all of it, then when the summer came round, my brother Felix and myself would cycle around to where Peter worked, and help with the hay, it would be gathered round into a circle, the idea of the circle, was to build what were called "cocks". After a few weeks it would be taken into the hay shed, or built in bigger stacks, that would be thatched and roped. My brother and I would have great fun riding on the hay cart. It was a special kind of cart, (it would only be the "bit better off" farmers who would have this kind of cart), it was very low, just one big platform with no sidings on it, you could tip it up by pulling a lever, there was pulley fixed to the front of the cart, it worked like a winch, the cart would be backed up close to the hay cock, then tipped up, where there were two wire ropes attached to the pulley. These were put around the haycock, and hooked together, depending on what make of cart. Some carts had a wheel to which a handle could be fixed, which was operated like a winch, others had two single levers, one each end, the pulley operated like a ratchet spanner, backwards and forwards. You could have one person on each side if you wished, that's when my brother and myself would come in handy, both of us would get on one lever, and someone else on the other one, we thought we were doing a great job. We also had great fun! I just hated the thought of going back to school afterwards I'm sure I would have liked school if conditions had been better but the teachers on the whole were a hard lot and we lived in fear of them. You cannot learn when you are scared! If you felt you were unfairly treated you were afraid to complain at home in case your parents went to the teacher and maybe make matters worse. So you had to just grin and bear it, I found it difficult to come to terms with all the changes - new school new teachers new family- I had to try and make new friends at school as well it was different from the school I had left because a lot the children there were neighbours but as time went by I began to fit in better and at home as well,

    Shortly after I arrived home my father's health began to fail. It had started to fail some time before my youngest brother Arthur was born but he kept on working wherever he could find work and work was very scarce. Everyone who knew him said he was a great worker and was in good demand if there was any work going he would get it. All this time he was suffering terribly it's hard to believe even in those times that he was unable to get proper treatment from a doctor, I don't know what the position was then as regards paying for treatment it is so sad that he had to go on suffering for so long I suppose there were plenty like him in those days so after a year and a few months he died and about three months before his death my grandmother died. It was one blow after another for my mother.

Then a few days after my Dads burial my three sisters Nellie, Florence and Agnes were taken ill with diphtheria. In those days it could be life threatening if not got in time. They had to go into hospital- my mother had to buy some new clothes for them- I don't know how she did it, but I remember her saying all the money she had on the night dad died was one shilling and six pence! When they were taken away in the ambulance to the hospital she said she thought they might not come back alive? Monaghan hospital where they were taken to, was thirteen miles away, a long way in those days with no transport.

If we were lucky a neighbour might be going with a horse and cart would give you a lift, it took a long time, but it got you there, and you would be very grateful for it, that's the way things were in those days, I remember a man coming to the house and lighting sulphur candles in the rooms I suppose it was to stop the germ spreading, anyway my sisters got alright and were out of hospital in a few weeks.

Now we had to begin the long hard battle to survive, we had a small thatched house with about three acres of land. No electricity or running water, well… not through pipes anyway, as it came through the holes in the roof instead when it rained. The room we slept in had an earthen floor which would become wet and soggy due to the rain coming through the roof. The beds were of poor quality- the bases were made of metal, angle irons ran up both sides and across top and bottom on which timbers or laths were laid across for the mattress to be laid on. In those days, these were known as a "tick" mattress. These were filled with feathers or horse hair, through wear and tear they needed replacing and we couldn't afford it so we had to resort to putting chaff that came from the corn after it was thrashed and cleaned. When corn was being threshed in the neighbourhood mother would send us with sacks to collect as much chaff as we could to refill the tick. However well it was done it was not very comfortable. As the timber was not fastened to the angle irons when you got into bed the timbers would move and the mattress or tick would go down through and look like a "fat belly" We had to get out of bed onto a cold damp floor to pull it back into shape. Sometimes you gave up and put up with it. We didn't have the money or means to make things better

Having a small farm was a disadvantage as we could get nothing from the state, I don't think it would have amounted to much anyway but any little would have helped, there was no one in the family working my sister Maggie who was the oldest was only seventeen, a few months before my father died she had gone to the convent in Monaghan to train in what was called domestic service, you needed to have this kind training to stand any chance of a decent job, such as working in a doctors house or any kind of people who were well off. The training was very hard but if you could take all they threw at you then you had a better chance of getting a job. People would go to the nuns and ask if they could recommend someone to work for them. My sister Maggie left the convent when our father died so she did not get her training finished. She needed a job now more than anything, a job came in a doctor's house in Cootehill in County Cavan and the nuns recommended her so she got the job but it did not make a big impact on our household income as Maggie was not good at holding on to money. She could never manage to save any money, she changed jobs a couple of times while in Cootehill but it never seemed to make any difference to what she contributed to the house. I suppose the wages were not very good anyway. After some time she went to Dublin to work, and then to England. I can remember some of the addresses of the places where she had worked in. She worked for a Mrs Goodrich in a place called Dawlish in Devon. Shortly after this, war broke out and mother was very worried. Sometime later things got more frightening when Maggie wrote, saying she had joined the ATS, in other words the British Army. This was very worrying to

Mother as she had a brother killed in the first World war, but thank God Maggie got through it all safe and well, and that is where she met her husband and he is still alive and well and a grand fellow. We were all a bit worried about what the people would say about her being married to an English man but we need not have worried at all as everyone liked him. He was quite good fun, especially when he would sing his funny Cockney songs. He got on great with everyone.

Cassie the second oldest in the family, a different kind of person from Maggie, Cassie, she was a real "go getter", she was full of drive, a great provider, if there were no sticks for the fire, she would get the hatchet and go off to the woods, which would be miles away, and come back with a big lump of a tree on her shoulder. Sometimes she might get chased by a farmer, but it would not bother her, she would never let go of the fire wood. We just had to survive. She was a very athletic girl, a great camogie player. She played for the local club Clara, which only lasted one season, as Clara and Carrickroe amalgamated and under the name of Truagh. They won lots of trophies in their first year and continued to do so over the next few years, Cassie also played for the county and won numerous trophies.

Getting back to the survival part, these were bad times made worse by political decisions. De Valera, who was Taoiseach at the time, decided to withhold land annuities which were currently paid to the British government, these were the repayments of loans which had been given under the various land acts to the small farmers to help them buy holdings. This was the start of what was called the economic war, the result of this was Britain stopped buying our farm products. De Valera was hoping the Germans would buy Irish farm produce, which was our main livelihood, but this did not work out and it was hard to get anyplace to sell our goods. You could sell your products but at a very low price and as a result smuggling came into full swing. There were some people who made a fortune at it. They would buy your cattle at a low price and then sell them at a good price on the other side of the border. I remember my mother went to ask a local farmer to buy a calf from her as she needed the money to buy clothes for my brother and myself for confirmation. She, almost had to beg him to buy, he gave her three pounds and ten shillings so we were well dressed on the day in suits and "Fred Perry shirts" that is what they were called at that time the little collar would be put out over the collar of the suit with the neck of the shirt open. We looked very smart. We travelled to the chapel by bus, it was my first time on a bus, my brother Felix and I did quite well. We got a good few shilling, people did not have much money to spare but on a day like that they would give children some money which would have to be handed over when you got home. I am sure everyone was much the same but we were a bit worse because we had no Dad.

Getting back to what I mentioned earlier, about it been difficult to sell farm products, the only way round this was to smuggle them across the border into N Ireland. This was not as easy as it would seem, there was quite a strong force of RUC police posted around the border town. My sisters Cassie and Nellie were very athletic girls and would smuggle the eggs into Aughnacloy which was in N Ireland and sell them there for a better price. They had quite a lot of success in dodging the RUC, but when you did lots of trips you could be unlucky? One of the times they were on a mission two RUC men confronted them a short distance over the border but they managed to get away. They ran all the way into Aughnacloy and sold their goods. When they left the place where they had sold their goods the RUC tried to grab them again, and again they gave them the slip, each of them taking off in different directions, Cassie ran down the Ravella Rd and jumped over a big embankment at the foot of the hill -at that time it would have been a good ten foot drop- and making it more difficult with a few strands barbed wire, she was been chased by a police sergeant called Holms, he was neither pleasant in looks or in character, he had a set of buck teeth and black moustache like an SS officer, any way looks were not bothering her, the main thoughts on her mind was getting back over the border and out of his reach. Nellie ran in a different direction, she ran up the town and over what used to be called the pound hill, and out the Augher Rd and then took to the fields and over the border, neither one of them knew if the other was captured. Cassie made her way back to Ravella Bridge and met up with Nellie again, in the meantime sergeant Holms had failed in his chase and made his way back to the barracks. A lot of people knew of what happened earlier and gathered to give him a bit of a hostile reception, the other police officer gave up the chase it has been said they enjoyed Holms making a fool of himself one thing I can say "they were a tough pair"

I have to say as well as being tough, Cassie had a lot of other great qualities, she was a very caring person, she helped me out lots of times, other people might not have noticed, but it meant an awful lot to me. One afternoon going along with her to the local shop which was called Mullins, we met the local Catholic Priest and he stopped and talked to us, he looked at me and said, "would you like to be an altar boy", of course I was surprised and delighted to be asked, not everyone got the offer to do this! The Priest had an arrangement that only boys who went to Killybrone School would serve the week day mass, as the boys who went to Aughamacklin School would not be able get home in time for school. He said you will need to get someone to teach you Latin, he said your older brother Packie could help you, and in a few weeks when it's his turn to serve you can go on the alter with him. When we got home Cassie said don't worry I can teach you the Latin, and I will take note of the things you have to do and when you have to do them.

Packie lived with our uncle Patrick and one morning during his week for serving one of the cows was sick! This meant that Packie would be delayed or might not make it at all, he asked me to go on and do my best, and that he would do his best to get there as soon as he could, so off I went and told the Priest what happened, he just said "go on and do the best you can". It was nearly half way through Mass when Packie arrived, and I had done everything right so far, never the less I was much relieved to see him, the point I am trying to make is the good job Cassie had done in such a short time. The Priest thanked me for the good job I had done, and asked who taught me, I said it was my sister he said she certainly did a great job, this all took place in the old church in Clara which was demolished in 1936, and while the new church was being built mass was said in the stable on the site –the new church was built on the site and opened in October 1938 by the Bishop Dr. McKenna a native of the parish, a lovely man who had a kind word for everyone. When the church opened I served the first mass with my brother Felix, Joe McMeel, Peter Sweeney and Jimmy Trainor.

Every year in the month of January we would have the religious exams in school, and the catechism would have to be all learned within a week or ten days. The teacher, Master Coyle, would have you learning most of the day. There might only be a few simple questions, but the teacher didn't want anyone to fail, more so for his own sake more than anything else, there was a big long table beneath the window which faced out to the main road, and alongside the table there was a seat where pupils sat for different lessons, he would have a pupil sitting on a chair on top of the table keeping a look out for passing cars, just in case it might be the school inspector, who would arrive most times at random. The teacher would usually make a run to get up onto the table to see for himself, it was surprising how fast he could move, he was quite a big heavy man, the children would have to move fast to get out of his way, if they didn't manage to get out of the way quick enough, he would use both hands to push them aside, he would just slide them along the seat out of the way.

All the children who would be taking part in the exams would have the work for their other lessons close by so as they could grab it if the Inspector arrived unexpected. The teacher had another side to him as well, if you met him after school hours he was a different person, he had a pony and trap, and would go into Aughnacloy from time to time maybe every few weeks, no set pattern, but of course it would always be in the afternoons or Saturdays.

My sister Nellie, my brother Felix and myself would go into Aughnacloy quite often, most of the times it would be just two of us, he would always give us a lift and give us a couple of shillings, and call us by our Christian names, he would be just like a different person, if only he could have stayed that way all the time it would have been great, when his own son Peter was at school he was a few classes higher than me, he gave him more beatings than anybody else,

Peter might have been a bit mischievous but no worse than a couple of other boys whom would be with him, if there was any misbehaviour, he would be the first to be called out, he would shout "come out here Coyle", the other two boys would be Vincent Macklin and Pat Sheridan but they would always get off lighter than Coyle junior.

    Shortly after this Cassie went to Killkeel convent, it was the same training course as Maggie had taken, she done her course, but I think she always had it in her mind to be a nurse, she applied to different places in England, and finally she started her training in Newport on the Isle of Wight. She did general and mental health, and she came through both courses with flying colours. She had a few very hard years training before becoming a qualified nurse, as the wages were not very good before she qualified, but she always managed to send money home. This helped a lot but still there was poverty! My brother Peter left school shortly after dad died, he would get the odd days work wherever he could find it, but every little helped. It's hard to believe that anyone had to come through times like this it was humiliating and distressing for children. Nobody had much but we always seemed to have less because there were more of us. I remember one time the teacher decided that everyone get together and buy a football there would have to be a collection for it everyone would pay three pence, or you did not play, and I did not have the three pence, so I could not play. However one day what seemed like a little miracle happened, my Uncle John came down to Dromore and he gave me a penny maybe the last one he had. I wondered where I would get the other two from. I went out to post a letter for the teacher, and there beside a stone was a penny leaning on its edge against the stone, what a welcome sight it was to me, it was like the hand of god put it there, so I got in for the two pence. I had missed the start [what a big deal], the price of a loaf at that time was four and a half pence, I had got over the problem of paying to play, no child could afford football boots in those days and the boots for school were not very good either it did not take very long for them to come apart, I would try and keep them out of sight of mum seeing them. Too much wear and tear might be the end of playing football. It was the only enjoyable thing at school

I had a good spell at school for a while when I was in the lower class we had a lovely lady teacher called Miss Smith known as Cassie Smith. I learned as much from her in that short time than I did in all the rest of my time at school put together, I would just hate to miss a day from her class, anyway the joy was short lived, and it was back to square one again when she left.

Times were still very hard for us, on days off from school if there was a farmer who needed some help at hay, corn, potatoes or whatever we would go and work for them. The money would not be much, about a shilling a day, but it was better than school, sometimes we would work several days without money, then the farmer would come and plough the land for us, so we put a bit of crop in and hoped that it would grow. I don't think that parents really understood what some of these people were putting their children through, driving them on to get everything they could out of them, but there was not much choice it was that or want and you would be in dread of getting the sack, so you tried to work harder than anyone else, but then you never got it easy at home either. There would be plenty to do after school especially in the summer time, there was water to be carried from a long way off in buckets for the few cattle we had, and also for the spraying of the potatoes there were weeds to be pulled and lots of other jobs to be done too.

CHAPTER 4

SOME RELIEF

At last a glimmer of hope, the government introduced the widows and orphans pension -which gave my mother thirteen shillings a week, this was a good help, but still not enough for a decent standard of living as each child left school this amount would be reduced by something like two shillings a week, there was never any thought of what it would be like when we left school. There was no hope but the spade as they used to say, even if you had plenty of ability there was nothing you could do about it, you needed money to go to a higher school, plus the fact that you were needed to earn money to help to keep other members of the family that were still at school.

Then my big day arrived, as I thought it was, my last day at school, the day I thought would never come, I thought I am free at last, but not free from plenty of hard work. The school leaving age was fourteen, I might not have got much home work from school but I had plenty of home work now of a different kind. My older brother Peter would leave a list of jobs every morning before he went to work, far more than I could ever do and well he knew it, then I got several weeks work such as tying corn, gathering potatoes and then I had a good spell pulling apples for a man called McClements. He owned a lot of land, forty acres of it in orchard, he gave quite a few people employment there. This would only last about six weeks. Anyway I got a job there, but it would be very cold on a frosty morning, or on a wet day when you got hold of the apple to pluck it, the water would run down your sleeve. You did not have to do this, you could go home if you wished, but you would only get paid for the time you worked, that was understood before you started the job, but he could be kind as well. I remember one very cold frosty morning he sent me up to the house to have a warm at the fire, and I suppose he felt sorry for me, as my legs were blue with the cold, I had to stay in shorts until I was fifteen and I hated it. I don't think my mother liked the idea of me becoming an adult too soon, but I was expected to work like an adult, and think like an adult, but be treated like a child, anyway sometime later on, I got temporarily upgraded to manhood, my Sister Cassie came home on holiday from England, and brought me a lovely pair of overalls they were the bib and tucker kind, the very best you could buy, they were my first long trousers, I thought at last I was a man, but not quite, I had to revert back to the shorts I hated on Sunday. I did not like being demoted every Sunday, Cassie kept telling mother not to do that. Sometime later I got back into the longs for good

My first real big job I did at home, was to set potatoes in the field which was called the back brae, that time every field would have a name, now a lot of those small fields have been put into one big field, anyway to get back to setting, mum decided this field would be ploughed, it was called lea ground. To explain what lea ground is, some of today's generation might not understand what lea ground is. It is ground that has not had crop in it a for a few years, there's not a lot of crop done in this part of the country now, normally the first crop would be corn, then flax, and then potatoes, then corn again. There would be grass seed sowed along with the corn, then the following year it would go back to lea again, that is how they used to rotate the land, as we did not have much land we could not always follow this pattern. With all the agricultural experts that are around now, I suppose they would think I was from another planet.

A man called Barney Flood ploughed the field for us. It took him two days, the fee was ten shillings per day, he could only plough downhill, as it would be too steep for the horses to plough up hill. I had to wait a while for the ground to settle before starting to set the potatoes, I had never done any setting before, but I had seen other people do it, I knew how to line the ground out into what was called rigs. The rig would be about six feet wide you could put three rows of potatoes across. The potatoes would be planted about 15inches apart length ways in the rig, some people might have four rows across depending on how big you wanted the potatoes to grow. If you had them too close the potatoes would be smaller.

To get started you put down two lengths of cord six feet apart then spread the manure between the two lines, we would mainly use farm yard manure with a little of what was called bone manure. Most people in those days would cut the potatoes into two or three or more pieces depending on how many eyes were in the potatoes, the eyes were what the buds sprouted out from and take root in the soil, and then the stalk would grow from that. The reason they cut the potatoes was more for economy than anything else but you needed to have at least one eye in each set to produce potatoes. There were always disagreements about the rights and wrongs of which was the best way! Some would say if more than one eye there would be too many roots and you would not have as good a quality of potato. Others would say to set the whole potato down was better, but if there was a lot of rain and the ground very wet, the potato might rot.

You had to dig a furrow down one side of the rig and repeat the same on the other side, and cover the potatoes with soil. Now this was all real hard man's work, and I was just a boy turned fourteen years of age with a very bad pair of boots without any socks, there was no point putting socks on because the soil would get through the holes in the boots and make matters worse. Every so often I would have to take the boots off and empty the soil, as we did not have a horse, pony, or donkey, I was all three, and surprise, surprise, we did not have a barrow so I would have to borrow my uncle Patricks. He would whinge about it every morning then let you have it, but it would have to be returned in the evening cleaned washed ready for inspection. OK it was just his way of going on, most of the land in Dromore was hilly, our house was on the side of a hill, to get manure out to the field from the "dohule" [manure heap], and I had to wheel a full barrow up a very steep hill over rough ground. A full barrow would be too much for me, it would have been more than a match for any able bodied man, but I had a great little helper in my brother Arthur. He was the youngest in the family, he was only a child, and not yet started school, he was of school age, but mum never liked sending any of us to school too early. Arthur was a very strong tough boy for his age, about 7 years, we did not have much to work with, not even a piece of rope. We used an old cycle tyre looped around the strut on the front of the barrow, he pulled and I pushed, he would run up over those rough stones in his bare feet, now this was real third world stuff or worse. I could not have done it without him or I would have had put a much smaller load on. The only reward he got was a ride back in the barrow and shared a bit of my egg at dinner time. I managed to set sixteen rigs, nearly half the field, this worked out well with mums budget. A man called "Pat the baker", Pat Treanor was his real name, he did a great job preparing, he made the ground ready, and opened the drills in two days, by which time I had finished setting my rigs. My cousin who was working in Tommy Brushes, asked his boss Tom if he would let him have the horses and carts for a day in order that he could draw the manure to the field for us, and Tom was only too pleased to oblige, the manure put in the drills and spread the potato sets were placed in the manure and the drills closed. The job was finished, and everyone did their bit, the world was very like that in these early days.

The potatoes I had set were starting to come up through the soil, it was time to start moulding them, this meant trimming the edge of the rig and digging the bottom of the furrow and breaking it up to make a nice fine mole. You then spread this over the rig carefully around the potatoes. This was called shovelling potatoes, one thing you were nearly always sure of, was that they would grow however wet the weather was, because they were sitting up high and dry. My first attempt at potato setting was a great success I was quite pleased with myself and I repeated the same process the following year with equal success it was a lot easier as the ground had been broken up the previous year

The spraying was another heavy hard job a forty gallon wooden barrel would be used for this purpose, you might have to carry the water from a long way off in buckets as it would be too much of a drain on the spring well, the well water would only be used for household use, so you would have to go to the little stream or an unused flax dam, there would be lots obstacles on the way to overcome. When you filled the two buckets of water at the stream or wherever you would be getting it from, it would be a good while before you would see much water in the barrel. The first thing you needed to do was to put a sack over the barrel, so it would act as a sieve to stop dirt getting into the barrel, and the nozzle of sprayer getting blocked when you filled it from the barrel. The spray was a mixture of what was called blue stone, there was about eight pounds in weight of this, and about ten pounds of washing soda. This was emptied into the barrel and stirred until it was all melted, then you put a piece of wood across the barrel to rest the sprayer on so as you could fill it up, and it was about the right height to get the sprayer onto your back and off you went, and let us pray that the heavens did not open up. There were no long weather forecasts then, if you got a sudden heavy downpour all your work would be in vain, and if you managed to get it done without it being washed away with the rain, the same process would have to be repeated in about two weeks' time.

Although some things had improved, the housing and living conditions were terrible, a lot of houses were thatched with straw, which came mainly from the corn, as there would not be much wheat or barley in those days. It took a lot of straw to thatch a house, and the farmer would have use to some of the straw to feed his stock, pigs, cattle, etc, people would have to use rushes which would only last a short time. Sometimes the wild birds would scrape holes in it looking for insects, or heavy winds would sometimes do damage, soon the rain would find its way through, then we would have what we called "down rain", you could be woken at night with the rain dripping on your face, there was not much use moving the bed, there were drips everywhere, and the rain that came through would stain anything it touched. It was like a sooty brown colour, so with earth floors in a lot of houses, there would be puddles of water on the floor and a damp musty smell. If you needed to go to the toilet, no indoor toilets at this time, you had to go outside whatever the weather, hail, rain, or snow, and there was nearly always one of them. This was all a terrible health hazard and Ireland was ripe with TB at this time and years before as well. Whole families were wiped out and not any wonder in conditions like these! Those who had money did not seem to care, the politicians looked after themselves, if you were poor you stayed poor, there was no way you could borrow money in those days, you might get a few shillings tick in your local shop if they knew you had something that you could sell, like turkeys or pigs or anything else that might be sold.

CHAPTER 5

THREATS OF WAR

AT THIS TIME, the dread of war was never far from people's minds, but it was only a matter of time before it would start, and start it did. On the First of September 1939 Hitler invaded Poland, I remember it well, I was tying corn for a neighbouring farmer called John Johnston, only a few people had a wireless in those days, my sister Nellie was with me on that day as well, we did not know until we got home, somebody got the news from the Priests house, Britain and France had declared war on Germany on third of September 1939, it was very sad that it took all that death and destruction for things to improve, there was more work, and more money, but food, clothes, petrol and most other things were very scarce, and rationing was introduced both sides of the border, a lot of people from Eire as it was then called, went across the border to work in Northern Ireland, the war brought many things, even some good, it kind of levelled things out a bit, because even if you had money you could only buy what you were allowed according to your ration allowance, but of course as time went on, what was known as the black market came into to being, and that meant that people who had money, could buy some the things on the black market, if you knew the right people there was a lot of dealing went on around the border, some things were more plentiful on one side, for instance tea was more plentiful in Northern Ireland, and sugar and butter was more plentiful in Eire, and so on. In Eire the bread was terrible, they used to say that you could kick it all the way home and it would not come apart. Local people from south of the border would go into the Town of Aughnacloy to try and buy some bread, sometimes without success, some of the shop keepers would not sell bread to us because there was a very heavy penalty for this sort of thing. There was a minimum fine of two pounds for one loaf of bread, and if you had a cycle, they would seize that as well, when I say they, I mean the RUC. Two pounds was a lot of money at that time, and the RUC were ruthless, we had what was called the special emergency powers act in Northern Ireland during these years, and it stayed that way for many years to come, so to survive they just took a chance, tough luck if they were caught. There was a man in Aughnacloy who had a little shop, he sold two loves to a young girl who lived south of the border, and he told her if she was stopped by the police not to tell them where she got the loaves, however somehow they tricked her into telling them what the man's name was. Arthur O Neill was fined twenty pounds and given a month in prison, that's how tough the law was. My own mother was stopped on the way out from Aughnacloy and the policeman wanted to take her back to the barracks and when she refused to go, he had to get a car to take her in, she wasn't going to walk, she was fined £2 and lost the loaf of bread. That's the way things were at that time!

The war brought death and destruction and all other bad things it brings with it, but I suppose you could say some good came with it, work got plentiful in Northern Ireland, there was compulsory tillage, a lot farm workers were needed, flax was a very important crop, so wages were a lot better, but had not reached their peak. At this time I had not yet moved to work in Northern Ireland I was working south of the border for what was still very low wages and working very hard,

I spent a very long hot summer working for a man called John Johnson in Killyhomen, he was a hard "hoor" as they used to say in those days, in other words he liked a good days work, but to be fair to him it was one of the few places where you were well fed, at the same time, every day you also had a starting time and a finishing time, unlike some farmers who would work away till it got dark. He was a good handy worker himself I learned a lot from him.

The "hay time" was hard work, every day in the blazing hot sun, the only machine we had was a mowing machine, it was pulled by two horses, all the rest of our tools were rakes and forks, all the meadows were low lying lands and flooded easy.

When the hay was ready for building, we would get a horse and hay cart, a hay cart normally was used for bringing the hay into the haggard or hay shed, but it was very useful for the purpose that we were going to use it for. As the hay cart was low and wide we could build the hay on it in the shape of a hay cock, there were no sides on the hay cart, it also had a lever on it which you pulled to tip the cart and slide the hay off without tossing it. This hay cock it would only be three quarter of its size. When we would have a few of these partly finished loads drawn in. we would bring in 2 or 3 more loosely finished loads, roughly enough to finish them all off, There would be two or maybe three ropes thrown over the cocks and tied at the bottom each side. While this was taking place the boss and I would be making ropes. These ropes would be made from hay. We would have a tool called a twister. There was quite a bit of skill in all this, the twister would be fixed to a small piece of hay that was operated by one person and another person plaited or "shaped" the hay into the form of a rope. When finished these ropes would be quite strong, these ropes were used for tying down the cocks of hay. Nobody ever explained why these lumps of hay were called "cocks", some people might call them rucks and I did not know what that meant either. In those days youngsters did not ask their elders too many questions you accepted what it was called and that was that. Building the cocks of hay would always be my job, it was a young lads job, but it was far from it, fully grown mans would be more like it. There would be one or more men pitching the hay up to you with pitch forks, they would have no mercy on you, your eyes would be sore with the sweat running into them, the hay seed would be down behind your shirt and in your shoes. Many years later my 2 sons would have much the same experience on top of trailers, drawing hay bales instead of cocks, during our summer holidays around Dromore, funny their tormentor was present at both episodes, Peter, but I digress. Sometimes I would take my shoes off, it was easier moving your feet through the hay without the shoes, but then it could be dangerous, as there would be thistle thorns which were not very pleasant and the danger of being stuck by the pitch fork. John Johnston himself was not too bad he would not overdo it, but there was another man who used to work for him, he would be doing his best to knock you over if he could, and have a good laugh about it, it was no easy task standing on top of a hay cock that had to be finished off into a pointed shape. At the top you would have to stand on one leg while you put little handfuls of hay underneath where your foot was, now if a grownup was doing the building, he would have a hay rake to steady himself otherwise he might fall off. This was not as difficult an operation as it sounds, the main purpose was to keep out the rain, and the lighter the person who was building it, and the better it was. When the person got off the top of the hay cock it would rise up a bit, this way there was nowhere for the rain to lie, the old men used to say that they wanted it so as, "the rain would break its neck off it", for all this I was getting seven shillings and six pence a week,

After the hay had seasoned a bit it would be brought into the haggard, the hay shed would be filled up first. The rest would be built in stacks, it was hard work for man and beast, whatever way you went it was up hill to the haggard. We would take in five or six loads, then build them in the shed or stack them, this would give the horse a rest, and then maybe you go to some other job that was more important.

You never ran out of work, even when it rained you would be sent out to cut thistles, and you would not have rubber boots or oil skins to protect you from the weather, your usual gear was a maize meal sack around your shoulders with a horse nail used as a pin to hold it on, and another around your waist. It kept out quite a lot of rain, there was always a good supply of them you could change when the rain began to come through, they used to say that between July 12th and august 12th was the best time for cutting thistles, there would be a hole in the stalk of the thistle at this time and the rain would run down to the roots and rot them. Anyway that was what they expected us to believe wet or dry there was never any let up.

CHAPTER 6

THE SLAVISH CROP

Flax was a very important crop during the war years, but unlike corn or hay, was the most slavish, You could work at it even in the rain, in those days it was pulled by hand, there were flax pulling machines, but they were never much of a success, it was a very hard to separate into chiefs or beets as they were mostly called, the bows which were on top of the flax fibre, that is where the seed of the flax came from, they were quite big and hard to untangle, unlike corn you could not bend it because it would damage the fibre, even if the machine had been successful, if the ground was wet the machine would get bogged down and cause problems, and you would finish up having to do it by hand anyway.

The farmers would seldom be able to be able to pay the men for pulling the flax for them, they would go around the neighbourhood and earn what they called swaps, they might need to go to ten or fifteen other farmers to get enough help to pull their flax for them, this system worked quite well most of the time. They would all arrange different days to suit each other, there would seldom be any problems, and they would have it all well worked out beforehand. It needed to work well, because unlike most other crops, it could not drag on for several days, otherwise it would spoil. When they finally managed to get it pulled, it needed to be put in water as soon as possible, although the rain may have been coming, pouring when the pulling was in progress, you still had to find a suitable water hole or dam as it was known to put the flax into, putting the flax in the dam would be described as drowning it, before the drowning took place a lot of hard work had to be done. The dam would usually be close to a river or some suitable water supply, the dam would usually be around thirty or forty feet long and eight or ten feet wide and about five feet deep.

We are now entering the flax pulling season, but unlike most summers the weather was very dry, as it had not rained for most of the summer, and water was very scarce, when the flax was pulled it would be put into a large dam which would be filled with water. In the majority of summers in Ireland, these dams would be nearly always full, they might need a little top up, and most of these dams would be close to a river, but Mr Johnston's was quite some distance away from the river, about a half a mile, this may not seem very far, but quite a way for what we had to do, and more so because, other farmers further up river would be doing the same thing as we were. First we had to put a barrier across the river, as the river was quite shallow, this would raise the depth of the dam so as we would always have the water waist high. There were two large high ramparts on each side of the river, this was to stop the river from over flowing and flooding the land around it. There was a little trench, which was dug out on top of one of the ramparts, which ran for about forty yards along the top of the rampart, then ran down a little trench on the side of the rampart, and then into a drain, which wound its way between different meadows towards the dam, then you would only need to dig a few shovelfuls to let the water into the dam, but getting the water there was easier said than done. Myself and another lad had to bail the water into a trinket (drain), which was on top of the rampart. The trinket continued down the side of the rampart and into a little drain which zigzagged its way along towards the dam. We had been doing this for a few days before any water reached the dam as it was a very dry summer. Mr. Johnson was a man that liked a joke about things and he used to come and say "have you been asleep or what?

As there's no water in the dam". On the afternoon of the second day he came round, and told us that the water got as far as the dam, and that little trickle had started to run into the dam, of course we wanted to go and have look, but he would not let us, he said it would be wasting time and by the time we would get there it would have stopped running, so we just had to go back to the human pump, for that's what we were. From then onwards he would give the odd word of encouragement, and we pushed ourselves harder to reach our final goal, but unfortunately the next morning there was no water in the dam, so off we went again with our buckets until we finely got it filled, even then it would lose water and would have to be topped up from time to time until it held its level, then the flax could not be put into the dam until it stayed full. Eventually we had achieved our aim.

Once the flax was in the dam no more water could be added to it. It had to be weighted down below the water, this was usually done by digging sods on the bank and putting them on top of the flax keep it underneath the water. The flax would be left in the water for eight or nine days depending on what the weather was like, if it was warm it took less time, or if it was cold it took longer. The reed of the flax needed to rot enough so as the fibre, which was what the linen came from, would separate easily when being processed in the mill, but first it had to be lifted off the ground and tied up in small bundles, or "beets" as they were usually called then. It would be stood up in little rows of four beets leaning against each other so the wind could blow through and it would dry out better. Then there would be four more beets put on top of these, they would be placed on upside down and would be opened out a bit at the top and spread round the ones underneath and tied together to keep the others dry. These looked like little tents and were called "stooks". When properly dried it would be built in stacks, and when there was a vacancy at the local scutch mill it would be taken there to be turned into linen and ready to be sold. Whenever your turn came round everyone would be trying hard to get done and sold before Christmas. When all the crops were done the boss John Johnson said that he wouldn't need me for a while.

CHAPTER 7

PETER JACK

I HAD WORKED for John Johnson from the month of May of that year until November which was 1940 till all the crops was saved, he already had another man working there full time, he said he would not need me for a while until some work came up. Then I had a few days at home, and there was always plenty of work to do at home, at this time my brother Peter was working for a man called Peter Jack, Peter Mc Kenna was his real name and would be called a few other names from time to time!

My older brother Peter was working for him at this time, but he caught a cold and I had to work in his place, it was only supposed to be for a few days but it turned out to be a lot longer than a few days, it lasted through the winter of 1940 until spring 1941, now I had worked for him before, but at those times there would have been quite a few other people working there as well, then he did not seem too bad, he was better when he had an audience, he could be quite interesting some times, he prided himself as been a great republican, but his attitude did not always live up to this, because the only people he allowed to hunt or shoot on his land were RUC and B Specials, which would not be the kind of friends republicans would have.

I found him to be a very unpleasant man, he did everything the hard way. I had spent a lot of time working for John Johnson, as

I have already mentioned, he was a very handy worker and would always show you the easy way of doing things, people used to say if you worked six months for Johnson you could go anywhere, it did not carry much weight with Peter Jack, in fact I think it had the reverse effect. Any work tools he had, such as a hatchet or a saw, would seldom be sharp, which made the work very hard, just imagine what it was like to saw through a tree about three feet diameter, it would usually be a beach tree which would have a lot of sap in it, unless the saw was sharp and the teeth set properly it was nearly an impossible task, but then the nearly impossible was something we got used to doing.

My work day started at eight am, I had to walk from home which was about two miles. When I got there my first job was to fodder the outside cattle, fodder means to feed. You would get a long piece of rope, lay it on the ground, bring the two ends together, then spread the ropes about a foot apart, and then put the hay on top of the ropes. But before you put any hay on the ropes, the boss man insisted all hay to be "bottled up", this was a special art. You lifted the hay off the ground with both arms reaching down in the same direction, with your body in a hunched position, you rested the hay across your thighs, then you caught hold of some of the hay on one side, and twisted it into a little rope, which you then wrapped around the bundle of hay, then you did the same on the other side of the bundle, and tied both ends together, this was not as difficult as it seems. In some places the bundles were called "bottles", in our part of the country they were called "wopes", anyway, you put as many of these on the ropes, then you put both ends of the rope through the loop at the other end, pulled it tight together, then you had to get it on your back, there was a bit of a knack of doing this, you lifted your load onto one knee, then you gave your load a boost with your knee and turned round quickly and got the rope over your shoulder.

You would have to do three of these loads in the morning and the same in the evening, now this time of the year there would be two horses standing idle in the stable, in normal circumstances the hay could have been taken to the cattle by horse and cart, there was no proper access to most of the fields and it was quite hilly ground, as well the holms were level but he rarely allowed you to fodder there, as there was no shelter. You would fodder them behind some bushes, somewhere you would have to get as close to the shelter as you could without the cattle seeing you, otherwise it would be impossible to get to a sheltered place before they tore the load of hay off your back, and if that happened he would have something to say to you, "and it wasn't what the rich called prayers".

Then when you finished with the outside stock, you then had to start on the inside stock, and fodder and water them. The water would have to be carried to them in buckets, and if the weather was cold each bucket would have some hot water added to it, to take the chill off it for the animals, never mind the poor child carrying it. This would mean that a very large pot of water would have to be on the boil all the time, then the byres (animal sheds), and stables would have to be cleaned out, and all this was done before you had your breakfast, hail rain or snow, and there was always plenty of all three of them in those days, but the animals always came first.

The boss himself would not get out of bed until between eleven and twelve noon, and then he would expect me to work to midnight with him sometimes, he had a horse drawn threshing machine, I suppose he considered it to be quite a modern day piece of equipment, as there were not many of them in that part of the country, there are still some remains of them about even today, the threshing machine would usually be situated inside the barn. There was coupling with cogs attached to it which stretched outside through the wall of the barn and this was fixed to another large cog wheel outside. Then there was a wooden pole or shaft, this is what the horse would be attached to, the horse would be driven around in a circular position all the time. There would be two men inside, one putting corn into the thresher, and the other one taking the straw back from the machine. This operation would very often take place when it was dark, he would have a hurricane lamp hanging up in the barn not the best of conditions for operating a threshing machine, it's no surprise that the amount of men that lost arms, fingers, or occasionally their lives in those days, there would be barely a little flicker of light shining through a little window in the barn so man and horse see could where they were going.

When the threshing was done there was a lot more work to be done. He would "bottle", or "wope" all the straw up, then all the corn would be cleared out from underneath the thresher, and piled up in a corner ready for cleaning. The corn would be put into an apparatus which was called the fans, the corn would be put in a chute on top of the fans, in which there was a sieve, this was moved backwards and forwards, the fans would blow chafe out the back way and the cleaned corn came out the front way. Now this sounds like it should be a simple enough task, but it was anything but simple. There were two cog wheels which engaged each other in order to operate the fans, but over the years a lot of the teeth on the cogs got broken on one of the wheels, which made it very difficult to operate, more so because if it was the main cog wheel that there were only about four teeth left on it, you had to go hell for leather to get any speed up so the wheel would free spin until it engaged the next intact tooth, it was real brutal work, you would have to change over every five or ten minutes and then it would not do a good job. He might have been better resorting to what some of the smaller farmers used to do, on a dry day with a nice breeze they would take the corn out to a field, put a cloth down with some hay or straw underneath it to keep it from getting damp. This cloth was called a "whinning cloth". It was made up of the sacks in which the maize meal came in. When the farmer would get enough of them he would sow them together and that was what the cloth was made of. This method was also hard work. You would get a sieve put the corn in, hold it up high with both hands and shake it, the chafe would blow away and the corn fall down at your feet on the cloth

Getting back to my boss man again, I think he helped to shorten his life with all the hard work he put himself and others through, during these war years there were a lot of subsidy and grants from the state. If the farmers ploughed some new ground that had not been broken for some years, they were entitled to so much per acre, well you could not blame anyone for trying to make the most of it! But the poor man picked the wrong kind of fields to plough. It was just impossible, there were beech, oak, and elm trees round these fields, and of course the roots spread a third of the way out into the field, anyway he started off to plough, but did not get very far until there was a big bang, the plough got bogged down under roots, one of the single trees had broken, the single tree was a part of the wooden structure of the plough, so he sent me up to the house to get a spare one that he had, and he said, "bring a hatchet with you to cut these roots, and tell Smith to make another single tree". Now this was a tall order as this man would never have the kind of timber available for this kind of job, by the way this Smith, was his brother in law, and luckily he was a very handy man and could do these kind of jobs, but could not work miracles. His name was Peter, but Peter Jack always called every one by their surname. Peter had a very hot temper and would fly into a rage sometimes, but he just was lost for words this time, he would take the hat and scratch his head, take a few steps and look at you and say "I give up", however after some thought he knew he had to do something. He went out and found a small ash tree, it was only just a sapling, it was nice and straight, and quite tall, he cut it into different lengths, for he knew it would be needed sooner rather than later, anyway, he did manage to make the single tree with whatever tools he got, perhaps he could work miracles after all. After sometime Peter Jack settled for ploughing the part of the field that had the least roots, he was running out of timber, and the plough shear was getting damaged, it had to be taken to the black smith every few days to be straightened.

Now for the next heavy task, at least once a week corn would have to be taken to the mill and cut into feeding for the animals, and this was a real brutal task and it did not have to be. In those days farmers would buy maize meal to mix with other feeding stuff, this would come in sacks of one hundred weight which was one hundred and twelve pounds, or eight stones, then there was the two hundred weight sack which was double the weight, he would always buy the large sacks of meal. When they were empty they were used to take the corn to the mill. He would fill them with corn, and ram them with a broom handle to get as much as he could into them, the corn being heavier than the meal, he could manage to get two or three stone extra into the sack. As a result the sack would be round like a barrel, it would roll about on your back, there were two lugs which enabled you to hold on to sack, this was bad enough to carry on level ground, but I had seven stone steps to climb. I went up these on my hands and knees as I was not able to lift my feet up onto the steps I would hang on to steps with one hand to help to balance myself. The mill man never made any offer to help, I don't think he was all that fit anyway.

It is hard to believe that things like this were allowed to happen. Nobody seemed to care, if you refused to do it and got the sack, how could you go home and say why you got sack. It would be such a shame on you, and no-one else would want to employ you. I was only sixteen years old just imagine what the effect it had on the growth of your body?

I worked for good men from time to time they would never let you lift anything that was too heavy, they would always say if you hurt your back, then it will affect you in later years, as I mentioned earlier, I worked for John Johnson he was a hard "hoor" but would never ask you to lift anything that was too heavy, Johnson was a very mischievous man. Well back to Peter Jack again, he would only shave once a week. He would go into Aughnacloy every Saturday night to McArees barbers shop to have himself shaved, He would take with him a large glass jar, which he would tie with a piece of cord to a walking stick and put the stick across his shoulder, he would leave the jar in the corner shop to have it filled with paraffin, which was used for the lamps to light up the house. It was always Johnson's intention to get some young lad to cut the cord and send the jar crashing, he always carried a pen knife which he used for cutting the tobacco for his pipe, he would be offering the knife and six pence to any lad that was brave enough to do it. His plan would be to keep Peter Jack talking while someone went around behind him and cut the cord, six pence was a half days wages for a young lad in those days. I am sure he would have raised it to a shilling if anyone had bargained with him, I can't recall anyone ever taking up the offer.

I have to say I did not enjoy one moment of my time working for Peter Jack, I think winter and spring were the worst times to be there, it was then that the sheep would start lambing, you had to be on alert all the time, there were all sorts of hazards about, such as the river, and rabbit burrows which newly born lambs could fall into. He would often take the lambs into the dwelling house to keep them warm, also when a cow would calve, the calf would also be taken into the house as well, and would be kept there for several weeks, and sometimes he would have two calves in the house at once. He would make up a little pen in the corner, he had two sheets of wood that he kept stored away for this purpose, one was nailed to the two legs of the table at the top end, which was nearest the fire, the other piece of wood was nailed onto table as well, wedged in the corner so it could not move, and this was the table where we had our meals. I don't know how his wife put up with all this, I don't know how she came to marry him, and she was a fine smart woman she was rushing about all the time like a servant!

As the weeks went by I was wondering when my brother Peter would be coming back to work or if he would ever come back? However the plan I had in my mind was when I reached the age of seventeen I would join the army, a neighbour of mine Pat Sheridan was in the Irish army, he was home on leave around this time I had a good chat with him about how to go about joining up, but it did not get to that stage as my brother Peter decided he was going back to work again, and he had a job lined up for me as well. I did not care what it was as long as I got away from Peter Jack's.

A man in Aughnacloy called Dominic McMeel wanted to cut some hedges and clean out some drains and get fields ready for ploughing, so brother Peter told him I could do the job, the pay would be a half a crown a day, in other words two shillings and six pence, I got on well with Dominic. Most places at that time would give you your food as well, and his mother and sister made lovely food, even though most things were scarce during the war years. I had known

Dominic quite well, he had done a bit of cattle dealing in a small way. He often came out to our part of the country looking for something to buy, he would buy a few animals in the south and smuggle them into north where he would get a better price for them. He was not always successful, perhaps he would not be careful enough at times, and the wrong kind of people would get to know when he would be going to smuggle his cattle across the border, and they would then tell the RUC, who would be waiting for poor Dominic. Informers or "touts" are despised everywhere but more so in Ireland. They would nearly always be known, and were lucky to escape a good hammering, Dominic was a good person and did not have a wrong turn in him. He was just trying to make a living by taking advantage of the situation. Nobody saw him as a criminal. It had a sad ending as he got caught once too often and got sent to prison for a spell. It seemed to take its toll on him as his health began to fail and he died at a fairly young age, but this was quite a long time after I had worked for him. I found him to be a decent man, he put me in touch with people around Aughnacloy who wanted their gardens done, so now I had more work than I could cope with. As soon as I done the first garden, next door would want theirs done and so on, I worked very hard to try and get as many as possible done, I was enjoying the work I was doing and I was being appreciated, then as I was about finished with the gardens, another man, Mr Elliot, asked me if I would work for him. He had quite a big business concern, he had a grocery shop and a public house, he also ran a small bus depot at that time, the buses would carry parcels to or from Belfast or any of the other big towns, and it was a quick and safe way to send a parcel. Getting back to his business again, he also owned some land, and kept a small herd of cows and delivered the milk to people in the town.

At this time Mr Lamb, his father-in-law, had handed over the running of the business to his daughter and son in law, Bob Elliot, and they were doing a great job of the running of it, they were all nice people, and I loved working there. My job consisted of different things, looking after the cows, bringing them in for milking, and helping with the milking, and putting them out again after milking.

The whole process we went through in the milking was so different from anything I had seen or done before, it was all so hygienic. Before the cows were brought in to the byres, the floors, they would have to be swept and hosed down, when the cows were brought in, they were put into a pen outside the byres where they would be left for about ten minutes until they relieved themselves, then they were taken in and washed down with a hose and then dried with nice clean cloths. Then the bucket which you milked the cows into would have a white linen cloth put over the top of it, which acted as a sieve, in our part of the country it would usually be called a strainer, this was to keep any foreign bodies getting into the milk. When the milking was finished the women would get the milk ready for delivery in the evening. When the cows were let out again, they were put out into the pen again for a while to do what they had to do, so as they would not mess on the town street.

My other regular job was delivering grocery and feeding stuff for farm animals to farmers out in the country, I did this with a pony and cart, it was a good going pony, the cart was well sprung with solid rubber on the wheels, we could fly along I was well able to cope with whatever job they gave me and got on well with everybody. Then one day Bob, the man who ran the business, asked me if I would like to have some time in the shop, and train to be a shop boy, that is what they were called in those days, of course I was delighted, those kind of jobs were not easy to get. He said it would be in a few months' time, after we had the hay saved and in the loft, I never said a word to anybody about this, if I had told Mum she would have been delighted, but when you are young it does not take much to change your mind, the hardest thing about this job was getting up in the morning.

During the war in Britain and Northern Ireland, the "summertime" time as we know it now, was kept on all winter, in other words the clocks did not go back at the end of one summer, then come the following summer, they put the clocks forward another hour, they called it double summer time. In Eire, where I was living at the time, there would be a few weeks when the times would change over, when

Eire would two hours behind the North, during this period I would start work at seven thirty, which would only be five thirty where I lived, I would have to get out of bed about four thirty and that took a mighty effort, we never went to bed till midnight or after, the rosary would have to be said every night before we went to bed. Sometimes I used to think it was a feeble effort, as some of us, including myself, would fall asleep, and you would sometimes get a rude awaking! My brother Peter would be up to his mischief, he would take a hot coal from the fire, and put at your bare foot! The best of intentions would be disrupted while you vented your anger.

One of the worst things in this job was, because I finished about five thirty in the north, when I got home at about four o'clock on our side, there would be another half days work waiting for me, the thoughts of joining the army would come to mind.

Saturday evening would be the one evening I would not go home early, a lot of the local lads would go into the town then, and we would all have a chat about different things, such as where they were working, and what kind of wages we were getting, I got talking to a neighbour man, Tommy Mills was his name, he said he was pulling flax for a man called Joe McGee, who was paying twelve shillings and six pence per day and he was looking for more workers. He said I could go out with him on Monday morning and see if McGee would take me on, he would meet me at Dromore crossroads about seven o'clock. I told him that I did not have a bicycle and if I was not there, not to wait, that I would catch up with me somewhere along the road. Now that I had made this arrangement I had got myself into a bit of a tangle, 1. I had not told Bob Elliot my employer that I was leaving, and 2, worse again, I had not told mother and this was going to be a hard one to get round, I would have to tell her in the morning, it was Sunday and there would always be more of the family around. Anyway I got around to telling her, she did not take kindly to this, to say the least, how dare I do such a thing without asking her first, she "hit the roof" as the saying goes, well the roof was not very high anyway! However things calmed down a bit, when I told her I would get as much for one day's work in my new job, as I would get for a whole week in the job I was leaving. She just did not believe that I would be getting that kind of money, for the six days I would take home three pounds and ten shillings.

Now I had my other problem to sort out, I had to tell my employer that I was leaving and this was something I dreaded. They were real nice people, I had to get it over with. I went on Sunday evening and told them that I was leaving, they were quite good about it, and when I told them the kind of money I would be getting Mr Elliot just said "good luck to you son, we can't match that, and we are sorry to be losing you".

CHAPTER 8

THE FUNNY SIDE OF IT ALL

Now I was ready for my new job with Joe Mc Gee, he was not a real stranger to me I knew him just by seeing him around Aughnacloy, in fact most people knew Joe Mc Gee, he had the name of being a bit of a wild man, my mother was not very happy at all, if she had known what others had put me through, he used a lot of F words. The first thing he asked me was my age, I was eighteen, then he rubbed his hand on my face, and with a bit of a smile on his face he said "you could do with a f@*%ing shave", then he said, "we'll soon see if you are any f#*%ing good", he said "get in beside Tommy, and if you can keep up with him, then you will do for me", then he went off somewhere for a while. When he came back, Tommy and myself were out in front of the rest of the men, I didn't like to be in this kind of position, I used to hear the men who had been pulling flax for a good number of years, that it was not the right thing to do, in doing so it would seem as if you were trying to show other people up, and that is one thing I would never do, even if I was capable of doing it, anyway, everything settled down all right, Joe was well pleased with my work, and I got along great with him. He said he knew me, since he had seen me driving Davy Lambs pony and gig. It was tough hard work pulling flax, on this job there was a funny side as well, there would always be a few characters who would be singled out for a bit of a laugh, maybe it was not right, and sometimes it would go too far. There was a man called Hughie, "Seamie" was his nickname, there would always be someone to pick on and get him all wound up. Although food was rationed the government gave the farmers extra coupons for their workers, so he provided us with food, we would have two breaks during the working day, the first around twelve noon, and then again around three thirty. We would all sit ourselves down using beets for seats, we would only be about settled down, when someone would call on Hughie to do a bit of a reel or a jig, and he would always respond, we would all start clapping the more we clapped the faster he went, then he would sit down to have a few bites to eat, and we would be shouting for more, he would do the whole performance, he would also sing and lilt, then maybe in the middle of it all Joe Mc Gee would arrive, and there would be Hughie trying to eat his bit of food, Joe knew what it was all about, he would start on Hughie by saying, "what the F#*%s going on here", Joe would then say "sit down and finish your eating, your no f#*%ing good to me when you're hungry, you will just have to work harder for the rest of the day". There was another man called Mick Collins working with us, he was a neighbour of Hughie, just to mention Micks name to Hughie was enough to send him into a rage, someone would say something that Mick was supposed to have said, then the slanging match would begin and that is how it went on.

Hughie must have been as strong as an ox, when he would be dancing and jumping about with all the weight of clay that was clinging to his boots, and the heavy wet clothes and how he could keep going for so long, the poor man never got any peace, he would take his bicycle to work, but someone would do something to it. He started hiding it at some farmhouse but someone would always find it, I used to feel sorry for him, it would go too far sometimes but at least he was well fed and was on good money. The food was much the same every day, but nobody was complaining about it, we were all very thankful to be fed so well in these times of rationing. Our meals were mainly white bread and butter and boiled eggs and a mug of tea, I would be looking forward to Sunday to be getting a few potatoes for dinner, in Eire at this time the bread was terrible it was called the brown loaf, but looked more black than brown, at that time some of the employers in the North would call the workers from Eire, "the hungry Free Staters". By now we had made good progress at the flax pulling, some of the flax that had been pulled earlier and put into dams, was now being taken out and dried, and getting ready for the mill. Joe took me away from the pulling, to help at other jobs, such as, the drowning, and taking out of the dam, and the spreading, and the lifting and taking into sheds at the mill. Although I was only lad, a lot of men I was working with were town people, and knew little or nothing about flax, Joe seemed to think that I knew enough to do things a kind of right, such as how long it needed to be kept in the dam, and knowing when it was ready for taking out. He asked me if I knew anything about when it would be ready for taking out, I said I knew a bit about it, and from then onwards, I was the one who decided when it was ready for taking out, the work was getting easier for me, but I would rather be with the crowd, it was a better craic. By this time the weather was better and the flax which was taken out of the dam had been spread, lifted and dried and ready to be taken to the mill to be skuched, Joe managed to get a man who had a tractor to take some of the flax to the mill for him, and this person would tip the load outside the door of mill shed. The flax would have to be pitched into the shed, and then pitched up onto the loft, a lot of the boys were from the town, and had no idea about using a pitchfork, so it meant that I was the main pitcher. It didn't bother me as I had done this sort of thing many times before, but we needed to keep on the move to get it all in before the next load came, otherwise it would have to tipped further away from the door, I did not know it at the time, but Joe was grooming me for bigger things, such as offering me a full time job, he would have me doing little jobs round the house for his mother, such as digging a few buckets of potatoes and milking a cow and all sorts of odds and sods. I know this was less slavish work but I would rather be out where the fun was, although I was quite happy whatever I was doing. One thing I was disappointed about, I had hoped that after my first week's wages that I would be allowed to get a bicycle. When I gave Mum three pounds and ten shillings she looked at me with a look of disbelief, as if to say "did you get this right", the next big shock was when I asked her if I could have a bicycle and the answer was no, and that was that. I was beginning to think I would have been better off staying in my last job, at least I would not have as far to walk and the work was easier, I was also hoping that I might get an odd six pence or shilling but no luck there either, I suppose every penny had to be accounted for in our household.

Then one day Joe asked me if I would like to work full time for him after the flax was all sorted out, he said there would be a big drop in my wages, I knew that was the way it worked in those days, you would never get as much for working full time as you would for part time. He said he would give me one pound and ten shillings per week and my keep, which would mean I would be sleeping there at night, it would have been an impossible task to walk there and back every day, it was about five miles each way, anyway when I told my mother, she said I could not take the job, because she did not want me staying away from home at night, I suppose she was being too protective, so I told Joe a little white lie, that there was too much work to be done at home, and as I was the only one at home, so he said to think about it for a while. In the meantime I carried on as usual. Then one day Joe asked me to go to a neighbour man, whose name was Tommy Montgomery, to tie corn. They would work amongst each other by swapping horses and machinery to help each other out. I suppose I was being sent to pay back one of those swaps. He would like to keep you on the go all the time, I only lasted a couple of days there, we were having our meal and I was sitting on some sheaves eating some bread and butter, a fly got in my tea and I was trying to remove it with a straw, Montgomery looked at me in a queer way and said, "don't worry, it's not Friday you can eat it". We were both of different religions, he was protestant and I was catholic so I took offence and threw the bowl of hot tea right over his lap. He jumped off the machine he had been sitting on and grabbed a pitchfork, which was enough for me, I took off and I was faster than him. Montgomery was the only non-catholic I ever had trouble with, most were respective of each other's religion. I was really worried that my mother would hear the story, she would not be happy with that type of behaviour. Luckily there was no one there that day who would have known who I was. The following day I did not go back to work with Joe in fact I never went back again.

Maybe it was the right thing to do, after all it was all very hard going, I had to walk six or seven miles every morning, and back home in the evening, and more than often it would be teeming down with rain, and yet they say, the sun was better then than now. I did not see it that way at the time, there would be days it would rain on you going to work, rain on you at work, and rain on the way home again, and to cap it all you would not any spare working cloths to change into, so the wet ones would have to be hung around the fire to dry and the fire would not always be of the highest standard, if you managed to get them dried at all, in the morning they would be like boards, you could stand them up against the wall, then give them a few bangs on the wall to knock the clay off them, then put them on you again, and start another new day.

On the day after I left Joe, I met a good friend of mine, his name was Peter Sherry, no relation, his brother Pat was married to my cousin Bridget, anyway we got talking, I had heard that he was working for Mr McClements in Garvey, I asked him if there was any chance of me getting a job there, and he said there was, and that he was looking for more men, he said get there in the morning and I'm sure you will get a start. So I got there very early in the morning, and Mr McClements said I could start straightaway, he knew who I was, I had worked for him before at the apple pulling, and he had known my Father very well, and he spoke very highly of him, my Father had worked for him a few times. He told me what the wages were, he said it was fifteen shillings per day, eight am till six pm Monday to Friday, I already knew all this, as Peter Sherry had given me the run down on things, I would be fifteen shillings a day better off, and have Saturday off as well, in fact in real terms, I was worse off in both cases, firstly "I" did not get the extra money, and secondly, I never got Saturday off, my brother Peter would always have a good hard day's work ready for me, that's the way things were at in those times, however, I liked working for McClements and most of the other people I worked for. In McClements the meals were at the same time each day, a good wholesome dinner, every day we got an hour for dinner from twelve noon until one, and fifteen minutes for tea in the afternoon, we would usually rush through our dinner to get out to lark about at some kind of games, one of the contests was two lads would sit on the ground on their backsides and put the soles of their shoes against each other the were then given broom handle between them to see who could lift each first, looking back now I think it was a good game to take part in, sometimes you would think you were going to get pulled apart, but still would not want to give in. Another one was to put a fifty six pound weight above your head with one hand, some of us were only young lads of sixteen years of age, it took a good while to build up the muscles for this, we got up to all sorts of games. Soon all the flax work was done, now it was apple pulling time, now this was quite a slavish job in wet weather, but it to soon came to an end. Then came the potato picking, now the evenings were beginning to get dark a bit sooner we had to finish a bit sooner. Mr McClements told everyone before the potato digging started that wages would be reduced to seven shillings per day, there were quite a few did not stay on, mostly people who had a good bit to travel, I stayed on as it suited me fine, I had only a short distance to go, potato picking was quite hard work but I had a good strong young back, and I had a great worker along with me. We worked in groups of two, with a large basket and a handle on both sides, the man who was working along with me was a man whose name was Patsy Rice we got on great together, Willie Mains was digging the potatoes, two horses were used for pulling the digger as the tractors were needed for other work, we were working on a big hill, so he could only dig going downhill and back up idle, this gave us a bit of time to get the potatoes picked up while he was making his way to the top again, every couple had their own heap for empting the potatoes, and of course your own space marked for you to cover Patsy and myself would always be finished first, but we would nearly always carry on into the others space to help them out, Mr McClements would have a walk around sometimes, he would always make some kind of remark like, "how come you two have the biggest heap? the potatoes must be better down here", but he knew what it was all about, we would have our heaps all nicely built up, we would have them sloped up like the pitch of the roof of a house, then the grass or rushes would be put over them, and the sometime later the clay be put over them, which kept them from the frost, in the process of putting the clay over heaps you created a small trench around the heaps, and little drainaway trench, to take the water away, this kept any water from getting into the potatoes. Anyway, I enjoyed working there, we all got on well together, I was sorry to see it all come to an end, but then on the last week I heard some good news of another job.

CHAPTER 9

MY DREAM JOB

My cousin Peter had worked for a neighbour man for a good many years, I used to think that if he stayed there till I grew up, if and when he would leave, I would love to take his place, and sure enough he called me to one side in Aughnacloy one night and told me that he was getting married, and would be leaving Toms and going home to his fathers to live, and do whatever work needed to be done there, and find some part time work as well. He asked me if I would like to take his place in Tom Brushes, he said he had mentioned it to Tom, and Tom said he would be very pleased to have me working for him. Then on my way home one evening from work in McClements, I was passing by Toms house, at times the river Blackwater would be too deep to cross, and one of the routes I would take would be past Toms house, I met Tom outside his house, he said "you know Peter is leaving, and he told me that you would work for me if I wanted you to", he said "Jimmy I am delighted that you want to come and work for me, but I will have to talk it over with your mother and see if we can agree on the wages and any other arrangements", he said he would come round on Wednesday night, which he did and everything was sorted, although I had no say in the matter, that was the way things were in those times, you were hired for six months, and you did not get paid until the end of the six months. My mother had told me before Tom arrived, that she could not agree to wait the six months without any money, Tom said he understood her position and said he would pay half the money in three months and the other half at the end of the six months, so everyone was happy.

So now I was ready for my new job. Tom asked if I would start in the morning, and mum said I could. He said he wanted me to go to his brother Willies house in the morning to help with the digging of potatoes. Willie lived just a short distance away on the other side of the Blackwater, unlike with many other jobs I had, I had no worries about being able to do this one. Although I was only seventeen, I knew I was capable of doing the job of any man, as I had crowded an awful lot of knowledge into those early tender years and gained lots of experience. It took about a week to get the potatoes finished. Now at last I was to go to my new place of work where I would stay for many years. I worked for Tom Brush for 12 years and 3 months and never had any official holiday, as it wasn't the way at that time, you were glad to be in work, but I got all the church holidays, which amounted to 10 days in a year. Tom was from a protestant family, but he knew better than I did when the catholic holidays were due. Nevertheless these were happy times, and I suppose if I had cleared off to England, I would have been a lot better off money wise, but I have no regrets at all, I am sure I would not have found the same happiness, I would have missed a lot of things that I enjoyed very much, such as the football, music, athletics and dancing.

Some people were treated very badly by their employers at this time, not a lot of respect, poor wages, poor food, and plenty of hard work. It was sinful how badly paid some people were, but my boss was not in the same category, many a time he apologised to me, to say how he could not pay me what I was worth, and referred to me as "THE BOSS". I took all the responsibility of the job and he trusted me completely.

Tom and Willie lived a short distance from each other on either side of the Blackwater, each had a horse, and the work that had to be done, therefore I worked with both as required. They had a rowing boat which they used daily to ferry back and forth as the work demanded. At this time Willie had a man working for him as well, he was a little man barely five foot tall, he was called Tommy O Neill, and he was a funny little character but a very willing worker. Tommy had come to Aughnacloy as a sexton of the Catholic Church, he first started working for Willie part time and then gave up the sexton job, and worked full time between the two brothers. There was a lot of farm work at this time during the war years, due to compulsory tillage. He did a lot of the farmyard work and helped with the tillage while I worked with the horses. Tommy was a very likeable person, he and I got on real well, I have a lot to be thankful to Tommy for, and if it was not for him I might not have learned to play music. Tommy played the mouth organ very well, of course I always wanted to learn to play some kind of instrument, at this time it looked like I would never be able to afford one, at that time there were no music shops around, I think Belfast was about the nearest.

Every so often Tommy would go to see his brother and sister in Belfast, so Christmas came around and off went Tommy, he had two mouth organs and he left one behind, so this was my chance to have ago at it. By the time Tommy got back I had learned quite a few tunes, I was not as good as Tommy but I was very happy. He managed to find an old melodeon which he could play quite well, I used to watch him play and when he went out at night I got hold of it and managed to get a tune on it as well, although some of the keys were not working on it, I really needed a better instrument. But as I said there were no music shops in any of the towns within reach of me, and my financial situation was poor to say the least, the only limited amount of finance I would have, would depend on how many rabbits I was able to catch, and up until now that was the only source of income that I had. This limited finance was used to go to the pictures three nights a week, apart from playing cards, which was the only kind of entertainment that was available around the neighbourhood and I was quite happy with it, but now I would have to improve my hunting skills!

At this time a neighbour and pal of mine, Packie McKenna, Peter Jamie was his nick name, was working for a man called Ritchie Falls,

I knew Ritchie quite well, as I used to deliver goods to his house when I worked for Mr Lamb, the big problem would be raising the money, my sister Cassie had told me if I saw an accordion for sale at a reasonable price that she would give me some money towards it, she knew that I gave all my wages to Mum, anyway my friend Packie got to know, that Ritchie the man he worked for, had an accordion and that he was planning to sell it, so I arranged to have a look.

CHAPTER 10

MY NEW FRIEND

Was not in the human form, it was a horse, my boss Tom and his brother Willie had a horse each which was a usual practice in those days, it worked quite well they were both very agreeable, but getting back to the horse again. The horse Tom already had was coming to the end of his working days, it was a good way to start a young horse off when you had him broken in to couple him up with an old steady horse, which would not get scared or too excited.

Tom bought the young horse in Ballybay, it was one of the main big horse fairs. It would be held on the third Saturday of every month, Tom and a few other men travelled by car, few people would have their own cars at time, it was war time and petrol was scarce. They hired what used to be called a hackney car.

In those times I would always go into Aughnacloy on a Saturday night, it was a kind of meeting place with other young lads, and it was the route they would take to bring the horses home from the fair, so I got myself in early to make sure I would be there before they arrived. Unknown to me, Tom and the other men had arrived in Aughnacloy quite a while before the horses arrived, there were quite a few horses, but only two or three men leading them. They were haltered together in little groups, I could hear the clatter of their hooves from a long way off, when they arrived they stopped near the top of Truagh lane as it was then known, it is known now as Ravella road, Tom and the men who went with him to the fair, were in a pub having a drink. They came out when they heard the horses, Tom had quite a strong voice, he shouted, "is Jimmy Sherry about anywhere", I was only a few yards away, I am sure he knew I would be there, so he asked me to lead the young horse out the road for him, and I was delighted to be the first to lead him to his new home, and the start of a friendship that was to last for years. It was also my home for many years, I took to that young horse straight away, I would always stay in Toms during the week but would go home on a Saturday, I did not want to go home on this Saturday, but I was around early on Sunday, put the halter on him, and took him for walk, he was such a lovely animal.

I was only a boy at the time, but I did most of the work breaking him in, but Tom would always keep an eye on things, and tell me what I should or should not do. He would put the harness on, and getting the horse to take the bit in his mouth would always be one of the first thing things you would do when breaking in a new horse. Then again you had to be careful taking the bit out again, sometimes a horse might hold on to it, and you had to be careful not to try and snatch it from his mouth, otherwise the horse would get frightened and back away from you, but these were things you picked up listening to men, and talking to those who had already broken lots of horses in, then the horse would be driven on long reins, to get what they called, "getting his mouth", this made this a very important part of the training, the reins were supposed act like a steering wheel, you pulled right rein to steer to the right, and when you pulled the left, the horse would turn to the left, it was very important to try and keep the same pressure on both reins, except when turning right or left. The next thing would be to get his shoulders hardened, he would be harnessed up with collar, hems and traces, and then hook the horse up to something light, maybe log of timber or a little trolley, you could add a little bit more as time went by until his shoulders got harder. After some time he would be coupled up with another horse to a plough or harrow for a few hours at a time. You would have to stop quite often and lift the collar off his shoulders and dry off any sweat that was on his shoulders, and let air move around the area for a little while, this was to prevent his shoulders from blistering. If the horse ever got blistered, you would have trouble with him for a long time, anyway everything went alright for me, and the last thing we harnessed him to, was the cart. The best time to do this was after a long day's work, some horses did not like being hooked up to a cart, but Dick, that was his name, did not mind in the least, nothing seemed to bother him, and him and me were becoming great friends, he loved being talked too, when I would walk past the stable at night on my way home, he would neigh, he seemed to know my footsteps, most times I would go in and talk to him.

This was one of the happiest times in my life for me, as well as having a great job, I knew everything about the place. I had been so many times as a young boy helping out with the work on the farm when Peter was working there, I knew every nook and corner of the place, every field had a different name, all the cows and horses had their own names, and the dog had funny name, I called him Spot when we first got him as a pup, but then Tom started calling him "pumpsey p", I don't know where he got it from, I gave up on spot after a while, he grew into a lovely dog, he was a half bred cocker spaniel a great gun dog.

When I first started working for Tom, I did not have a gun licence, as well as a licence you needed a firearm certificate, to keep or carry a gun in and around your own dwelling, which only allowed you to shoot or to scare vermin. It was a bit of a drawback to me, as I had to give all my wages up, I needed some means of earning a few shillings. I used to snare and trap rabbits and sell them for ten or twelve pence, there were 12 pence to the shilling in those days. I used to like to see the Blackwater in flood, because that's when I was able to use the gun with much less risk of getting caught. Where we lived would be completely surrounded by water, so the police would not be able to get near us, the rabbits had their burrows near banks of the river which would be flooded, so they were flushed out into the open, you could stand there and pick them off. It might seem cruel, looking back at it now, but it was all part of survival, if I did not do it someone else would. It was war time and food was scarce and the rabbits were a source of food, and they did a lot of damage to crops, but eventually I applied for and got my gun licence.

    I suppose the border between North and South was maybe a bit of a blessing at times! There would always be someone from time to time looking for a hand with something, one time it might be to help to drive some cattle across the border, and as certain things could be scarcer in either the North or South, or somethings could hardly be had at all. Tea was scarce in the south- you were only allowed a half ounce per person, while in the north it was two ounces per person, rationing was in operation both sides of the border, sugar was quite plentiful in the South so there would be all kinds of wheeling and dealing going on, sugar for tea, and lots of other items. I think bread was one of more important things, the bread in the South was terrible, it was supposed to be brown bread, and we were told it was healthier for us, but if you believed that you would believe anything, bread smuggling carried a heavy penalty, a minimum of two pounds sterling fine per loaf, and they seized the loaf and whatever means of transport you had, two pounds was a lot of money in those days. This border patrol was done by the RUC and they were quite a nasty lot, there are lots of unbelievable stories, too many to mention all of them.

    One time my mother was stopped by the RUC, a short distance from the border, the officer who stopped her was on foot patrol, she had a loaf of bread with her, and the officer seized the loaf, and told her she had to go back to barracks with him, which she refused to do! It so happened my brother Peter, God rest him, was working in a field right beside where she was stopped. He was working for a woman called Mrs McKenna, who was the wife of the late Peter McKenna, known as Peter Jack, his land was in the town land of Ravella, and it was on the Ravella road that all this had taken place. The policeman knew my brother, and he ordered him to go into the police barracks in Aughnacloy, and tell them to send out a car, so as to take his own mother into the barracks. There was a very heavy penalty for refusing to carry out this order, so he had no other choice but to obey the order, this was a time of war, and there were a lot of strict laws in operation it was easy enough to get yourself locked up, especially if you were catholic.

There was a man who had a little shop in Aughnacloy his name was Arthur O'Neill he sold lots of items like confectionary whenever it was available, as everything was on ration, he also sold bread which was not on ration, but he was not supposed to sell it to anybody from Eire, it was not always easy to know where people came from, and it was not a nice thing for a shopkeeper to have to ask people where they came from, however Arthur was unlucky he sold two loves to a young girl from Eire, she was stopped by the police on the road near the border, they asked her questions in such a way that she might give away where she had bought the bread, and she told them and she bought it from Arthur O Neill, so Arthur was taken to court, sentenced one month in prison, and fined twenty pounds. It was a harsh sentence for such a minor offence, this was only one of many similar things that happened on the border in these times, which I will get back to later.

Tom my boss was easy going, but the work was there to be done, and I had to do it, there would be days when I would not see anyone except Tom. But when there was extra work to be done, we would join together with his brother Willie who had a farm on the other side of the river and help each other out, this arrangement worked quite well. In the springtime I would be out in the fields working with the horses, sometimes as much as a mile away from the house, I did not have a watch in those days, there was always some guide line you could go by, such as the sun shining through a certain gap in the hedge, or over a certain tree, but the best guide was the Angelus Bell being rang in Clara Church, it would ring at eight am and twelve noon and six pm in the evening, Aughnacloy church was much nearer to us, but bells were not allowed to be rang in Northern Ireland during the war. The horses would know when the twelve noon bell rang that they would soon be getting a break, Tom would bring me something to eat at noon, and again at six in the evening which was finishing time, I'm sure that the horses were wise to all this, sometimes I had to stay a little bit later to finish something off, and you could tell the horses did not like it one bit. They knew all the sounds, Tom would always call me for my dinner, it was a call that Tarzan used to make, they would know that sound as well, I loved working with the horses they were great company, often they would be the only company I would see all day.

The flax pulling season began in the late summer around August time, Tom would have a field of flax for himself, and he would give me a field for to grow flax for myself as well, but it would not really be mine, it would my mothers, or most of time it would be my brother Peters. There was also another man who would sometimes have a field for flax as well, his name was Mick Keenan, and he was very tall man he would be known as big Mick, this was one of the very busy times of the year as it was also hay making time. We managed quite well most of the time. We would each fix a day for pulling our own flax so as it would not clash with each other's program, and if needed we could all help each other out.

There was a lot of preparation to be done before the pulling started, the dams would have to be got ready, and make sure they would hold the water to drown the flax, this was known as dam rotting. It was hard work but a lot of fun as well, there would be all sorts of discussions and ribbing each other, however the work would get done eventually, then the rest of the harvest would have to be done, and soon winter would be upon us and the mad rush would be over for another while.

CHAPTER 11

A CHALLENGE

During those years there were a lot of grants for land clearing and land draining and so on, at this time Tom had some land which was overgrown with bushes and trees, Tom asked me if I would be able to clear one field for him in the winter time, when the crops would be all gathered in. Now this was a real challenge, and I always loved a challenge. Now at this time Tommy O Neill was still working for Tom's brother Willie, as Willie did not have enough work for him it was arranged that he would come and help me. Tom said it will be a mighty big job, and he said its grant money from the Government for doing it, and so I will share that with the both of you, and that was great news for us, so we could not wait to get started. As I said early on, Tommy was a small man but very willing and was a great help to me, he loved the glory of it all, he would go over to my cousin Packie Sherry's house and tell him how well we were getting on, and Packie would say to him, "I can't see anything being done", Tommy used to get upset about this, for the reason he could not see anything done, was because we were in a corner of the field and the view was shaded by hedges and trees of the surrounding fields. It was several days before we could be seen, we did not have a lot of tools, a couple of billhooks, and another implement, it was called a stubbing axe, also crosscut saw, a couple of pitch forks and a few other tools. The one thing that would have made it easy for us was a tractor, but we did not have one, or even a hand winch would have been a great help, we could have put a chain around the small bushes and pull them out. There were some good sized trees to be taken out as well, so we would dig around the bottom of the tree, cut the roots, we then put a rope on the tree and pull it down by hand. Tommy would cut all the branches off the tree, while I would be stubbing some other smaller bushes. Tommy often would brag how he would never break any of the handles in any of the tools. One day I could see the billhook I was using was beginning to get the worse for wear, so I put it down leaving it handy for Tommy to pick up, and sure enough he did, he used it for a good while before it broke, well he did not know what to say for himself, as his pride was hurt, but there was worse to come, he lifted the other billhook and started using it, and after some time it broke as well, and I had not seen any faults in it, so now things were looking bad for poor Tommy, I was splitting my sides laughing, however there was a helping hand not far away! My cousin Packie was the handy man for the neighbourhood and he worked for free, I often told him if he had been a mason he would be called a freemason, and indeed he was good at masonry work as well. Tommy arrived at Packies that night with the two billhooks to get new handles in them, and Packie being the man he was, managed to get one of them done that night, ready for action next day. Before long were out in the open, and the neighbours could see how we were getting on, eventually we got the whole job done in three months. Looking back now, it seems hard to believe that two people could clear all that with very little tools Anyway the field was ploughed and flax sown on it, but it did not turn out very well that first year, really the ground would have needed to be rested for about a year without putting any crop in it, however Tommy and myself did not do too bad, Tom shared the grant money with us and it helped us a lot. After a few years we cleared another field, but it was a lot smaller job, it was ploughed and flax sowed on it, and it turned out quite well.

Summertime was always exceptionally busy, there was always hay to be cut. Without boasting I was always the one to go over the top when the weather was good. I would be at work from dawn to dusk. I never liked working the horses in the blazing sun, I would start work about 4.30 am before the sun would rise and get hot. I always thought it cruel to work horses in the blazing sun, when they would be eaten alive by flies. In getting the hay cut early in the morning it gave us a full day to get the hay gathered and built into cocks or stacks. We had to make our own ropes with an implement called a twister, you needed two people for this, one to twist the hay, and the other to feed the hay into the shape of the rope, this was to tie the cocks down, so the wind would not blow them away.

Sometimes the hay was too dry, so we had to gather it into a circle where we were going to build it and when the sun went down we had to build what we had gathered, as long as needed, often way into the night, and your eyes adjusted to the fading light. We benefited from the hard work, and had the hay saved before others were thinking of starting. We then had to get it into the sheds as soon as possible as we were on low lying land which was liable to flood. When the hay was sorted it was time for the flax to be pulled which could be done even in bad weather. Flax was put in a dam filled with water –this process was called dam rotting, and left there for 8 to 10 days depending on how hot the weather was and then it was taken out and spread over a cut meadow and left to dry It was tied and put in a stack and later in the year taken to the skutch mill and turned into what is called Linen. This was used mainly for making parachutes for the army, and clothing.

All the crops were nearly ready for harvesting at the same time, so it was one hell of job to keep up with it. now at this time there was double summer time in Northern Ireland it would start around the end of April and finish about the end of September then after a short time passed they extended it to a longer period, then there would be a time at both ends of the summer when there would be two hours difference in times between North and South it was all quite strange if you lived near the border, if someone asked the time you would have to think where you were. They would ask you which time, mad time or ordinary time. Mad time is what they called summer time south of the border.

Living on the border at that time must have seemed a bit mad as there were so many rackets going on! Some things would be higher priced on one side than the other, just as happened to my mother and the loaf of bread. I could earn a few shillings by helping some people by carrying things over the border. There was a risk both sides the RUC in the north, and Irish customs in the south. I had many a scare, many a laugh and many a tumble over a ditch. I remember helping to drive some cattle towards the border one night when a car came in sight, I jumped over a hedge thinking that the ground on the other side would be the same level, unfortunately it wasn't, so and I got a shock as I seemed to be falling forever. When I did land it was on a very steep slope and I rolled through briars and bushes before I came to a stop. I was well used to these sort of things; if only they had camcorders in those days, we could have had our own movie industry. They were all first takes or stuntmen.

I recall another time a few of us were driving some cattle through meadows in the long grass, there was a small little man helping, his name was Earnest Varner. He just suddenly disappeared, leaving the hat sitting on top of the grass, a few seconds later the head reappeared in the hat, he was not hurt so it was a good laugh, he had gone down a deep hole in the ground which led to some underground pipes, it was just like shot from a laurel and Hardy movie, these were just a few of the many things that happened. I recall another venture maybe not quite so funny, my cousin Patrick Sherry asked to give a hand to carry a pig that he had slaughtered, prepared and gutted for the market. The plan was to carry it as far as the Blackwater River, which roughly marked the border near home, then it would be my job to carry it across the river, and I would take it to the market in Aughnacloy the next day, as you would get a better price in the north. My employer would claim it as his, in case any questions were asked. I had long pair of waders which reached up to the top of my legs, there had been some heavy rain and the river had risen a little higher than it normal, which caused it to flow faster which made it bit more of hazardous to walk, you didn't have much room to bend your knees! It was Patrick's job to pass the pig down to me in the river. The bank being very high it made it very difficult to pass the pig from one to the other, somehow or other he lost his grip too soon and the pig landed in the river. It was panic stations as it started to float off, so I had to run after it through the water. Patrick shouted at me to let go or you'll drown yourself. I managed to get hold of it eventually, it was full of water and had to be emptied out as it was 200lbs weight without the water. I stood it on its head and managed to empty it, I put it on my shoulder and carried it across the river. It wasn't funny! Patrick had fed the pig for three months expecting to use the money to feed his family, and we weren't going to lose it to the river, so thanks to my determination, Patrick got his money as planned from the sale.

I'm sure a lot of stories could be written about the border especially during the war years, the law was very strict on smuggling and "black-market" but we never looked on it as criminal. If there was something you could not get on one side you could get it on the other and pay the penalty if you were caught. It was a minimum fine of £2 if you were caught with a loaf of bread and if you had a bicycle it was seized as well. It was usually the locals who were caught with a few things for their own use what I am going to say now may seem hard to believe.

During the war a lot British and US soldiers were stationed in Northern Ireland, the US soldiers would be called Yanks or G I's, the Brits would never have as much money as the Yanks, and could not afford some of the little luxuries that could be had, if one knew how to go about it! Things such as chocolate, alcohol, and various things that could be had south of the border. Certain men took advantage of this and sometimes the Yanks would get ripped off, maybe not the right kind of stuff in the bottle, drinks that looked like whiskey but wasn't! There was one fellow who was a decent honest man, he got to know what the needs of the Yanks were, he had it well organised, he would buy the goods south of the border, or wherever it was available, get in touch with them and stash it close to the border in the south. Then he would meet them at a certain spot north of the border dressed in an American uniform, they would drive towards the border, pick up the goods and be on their way. He got his money, changed back into his own clothes, and got on with his life until the next time. He never had any trouble with the RUC because they were not allowed to interfere with the American forces.

War is evil and terrible, but a lot of people made money from it. People wondered if it would ever end! One old man used to say, "We'll all wake up one morning and there will be German tanks all around us". But that didn't happen thank god.

CHAPTER 12

THE WAR ENDS

The war finally came to an end. It did not make much difference to me as whatever I earned had to be given to my mother, this would have been the right time to emigrate to England or the USA. There was great money to be made in England after the war but my mother never wanted me to leave Ireland, I suppose she liked to have me under her control. That's the way it was at that time, and I lived and worked north of the border until I left for England in 1953. I suppose I was better off living and working in the north, but conditions were the same all over rural Ireland. There was no electricity or running water, at least not out of a tap, there was plenty of running water coming through the roof and down the walls, neither were there many houses with inside toilets, not even what they later called a "helsen" bucket. The helsen bucket was a bucket with a lid and a handle, this was placed under a board fixed to the wall, with a hole cut in the middle. You could lift the bucket out when full by the handle and empty it in a hole dug in the field. Not everyone had this facility so they had to "go" behind a hedge somewhere, where no man ever went before. We were lucky to have this bucket as my sister married an English man and it would have been improper to have him "going" behind a hedge. I remember when my sisters had to go and buy toilet paper, and they went the 13 miles into Monaghan town, as they were too ashamed to ask for toilet rolls in the local shops. Anyway the whole process was an improvement. It was better than an open field on a cold rainy or snowy night. Other washing facilities were a big problem, more so on Sunday morning when everyone was trying to get ready for mass. It is hard to imagine what it was like for the family, 3 girls and 5 boys at this time, all trying to get washed at the same time. There was not a big supply of wash basins, towels or mirrors, and the water had to be carried from a well quite a distance away.

I was always the one to adapt to these situations as I only stayed at home at weekends, I would be up before the rest of the family on a Sunday morning, boil some water for shaving, find a bucket or bowl, and providing the weather wasn't too bad, I would shave outside. I got myself ready for mass, had my breakfast and went on my way. I would set the bucket on a stone seat which was beside the garden gate, and not far from the window, which I used as a mirror. I got the whole thing over as quickly as possible, and was finished by the time the rest of them had finished arguing about it. My older brother Peter would get the first choice, but we would all have to get to Sunday mass whatever else happened.

Of my sisters that remained at home two of them were in apprenticeships so Agnes was left to do all the work about the house. The water for washing the clothes had to be boiled on the fire and working, football and running garments had to be washed by hand in a tub, and it was never easy to get them dried. They had to be ironed, no electric iron then, the iron that was used consisted of two triangle pieces of metal which were heated in the fire, the base of the iron had a hatch which you lifted up, and you picked one of the pieces of metal with a pair of thongs and placed it in the iron. During ironing as the plate began to cool down, you put the first plate back in the fire, and used the other one, and so on until the ironing was done. Then something super came on the market, a "Tilly iron", which made the job easier. It was the same idea as Tilly lamps, which were common in homes and country dancehalls at that time. No rural electricity was available at this time and being a border town we were one of the last counties to get electricity.

Peter Sherry (My Father)

James age 7 at Carrickroe School 1931

Mum & Arthur

Sherry Family (circa 1936)

Sherry Brothers

James in front of old house

Crane Crook

Eugene O'Neill (taught me how to play melodian)

Working in the flax dam

Jimmy, Mum, Nellie & Packie

Glaslough Harriers 1948 (Jimmy 2nd from left, Felix 2nd from Right)

Clara Band

Clara Band marching

Hugo & Jimmy with Bread van

Princess Maud

Pat Sheridan, Jimmy, P. McKenna & Joe Woods(L-R)

With Felix(Brother) on Berry Wiggins

Jimmy on top of oil tank on Isle of Grain 1965

Jimmy with Kevin Cochrane

Peter (brother), Jimmy, Paddy McCarron, Arthur Sheridan (L-R)

Dromore New House.

Working with Arthur (brother) 1986

Sherry Family (circa 1990)

Gigging with Christy O'Brien (L) and female singer

(L-R) Genie O'Driscoll, Genies wife, Jimmy, Mary Connolly, Arthur

CHAPTER 13

THE WINTER OF 1947.

It started to snow on first few days of February, it had been freezing hard for a couple weeks, and the ground was rock solid. The Blackwater was frozen over, it was starting to snow when we got up in the morning, and it snowed heavy all day and all through the night. My main concern the next morning was for the cattle outside, they were out in the open and it was most of a mile to take the hay from the shed to the cattle. I could not use the horse, because the "frog" of the horses hoof would fill up with snow and become like a football, and the horse would break his legs. Even without that danger it would have been imposable, as there were lots of deep ditches, and no way of knowing where they were. There was only one way, and that was to get a rope, and put as much hay in as you could carry, I managed to get the rope full of hay on to my back and headed for the cattle.

The snow was so deep that the hay was dragging on the snow, I would have to stop and try and clear the snow off the hay. I knew the land like the back of my hand, but it was still a very difficult journey, because if you missed any of the bridges across the drains, you'd be very lucky to ever get out alive. At last I found the cattle, they were huddled up together in a bunch, you could just about see their backs, and their bellies were resting in the snow. I divided the hay amongst them and went back for more. When I returned they had eaten the first lot, luckily we had a hay shed, so it made it a lot easier to pick the hay up. Now I had to turn my attention to the cows, calves and horses that were inside, they were bawling their heads for their feed. As I came to the farmyard, I could see this bit of hay moving along the top of the snow, it was wee Tommy O'Neill trying to make his way to the byre to fodder the cows. He would have been better to get a shovel and make himself a path from the byre door so he could get the door open. He had put the hay down and the wind blew it all over the place. We managed to get all the animals inside fed, we had to leave the watering of them until later, as neither of us had yet had any breakfast, but I could smell the welcome smell of bacon. When we got indoors there was a big roaring fire going, and Tom had the breakfast ready. When breakfast was over, now we had another big task on our hands, and was to get water for the animals, as I mentioned earlier the Blackwater River was frozen over, as were all other water supplies, in normal times we use the water that fell on the galvanized roofs of hay sheds and all the other such roofs. We would have a few forty gallon barrels to catch the gutters off the sheds, but they were all frozen up as well. Now the river was the only option, it also left us with a longer journey to carry the water, so wee Tommy O Neill and myself made our way to the river. We knew the river was frozen, but still we had to be careful in case there was weak spot in the ice, we soon found out there were no weak spots, and getting some kind of a hole broken in the ice was going to be a big problem. We tried a few different tools without much success, so then we tried the chopping hatchet and it was a lot better, but it still took a long time to get a break through the ice, the ice was about nine inches thick. We finally got a hole made big enough to get a bucket through, the level of the water below the ice had fallen as the river continued to run, but the ice sheet now was forming a bridge from riverbank to bank. We had tie a rope on the bucket and drop it down into water, there was nothing easy about this job, there was quite a steep bank which we had to climb up to lay our buckets on level ground. We could only take one at a time, as you needed one free hand to steady yourself, by the time you got one bucket to the top and got back down to the river, there was layer of ice on the water again, and looking back now it takes a lot of believing. We had two big buckets and two small buckets, as Tommy O Neill was a very small man, he was known as Wee Tommy but a very willing worker.

While we were busy doing all this, our Boss was busy with another project. We had a 40 gallon boiler up in the yard, which was normally used for cooking the feed for the livestock, it was heated by firewood or whatever was available in a firebox underneath. The water was too cold for the cattle to drink, so we had to fill the boiler and boil the water, and by the time we got it to the cattle the water was cooled. Before we could get the cattle watered properly we needed the snow to be cleared away so as the cattle could move. Now this was going to be a mighty job, so I got myself a large shovel and headed towards the cattle and started digging until, I had the size of a small room cleared, then I cleared the snow completely around one animal, and moved into the spot that I had already cleared and hoped the others would make an effort and follow which they did, I am sure it kept them from freezing. I kept on digging for hours, until there was enough room for them to move around, by the time I had finished there was a wall of snow about nine feet high and it was quite warm inside out of the wind. We were beginning to get control of things, but one never knew what was coming next, this might seem a strange thing to say, but I was glad it was still freezing hard, because the snow got frozen it would not drift, and would keep the shelter clear. All this was happening on the same day, but we still had to get the water to the outside cattle, and even if we did manage to get water to them, how were we going to water a herd of cattle with four buckets of water at a time, this would be an impossible task. So I came up with an idea, we had two empty forty gallon barrels, which our boss cut in half for us, while we were busy doing other things. then we were able to drag the half barrels along the top of the snow to the cattle shelter, then we cut some empty sacks and tied them over the tops of the barrels and poured the water through the sack into the barrels, so the cattle could not get to the water before the barrels were full, and the sacks were removed, it took a long time but we got there, but it was not long before we had to start the evening feed again. Water had to last till the next day when I was able to borrow what was called a creamery can, it held ten gallons it also had a lid on it. I could put it up on a platform and fill it, it had handles on it, and I tied a rope through the handles and carried it on my back, but I could not put it down till I reached the cattle, it would be too heavy to get it back on me again! Anyway that was day one over.

We were getting low on feeding stuffs for the cattle and we needed household goods for ourselves. After the animals were fed the next day, Tommy and I headed for Aughnacloy for some feed for the animals. We had some empty sacks with us, we brought one hundred weight of feed stuff for the animals, and this was another hazardous journey as the roads were barely passable. We had to divide the bag of feed, I put about a quarter of the feed in a separate bag for Tommy to carry, and I carried the rest of the bag, the road was very dangerous it, was just a solid block of ice, rough and bumpy, something like you would see on one of those Attenborough arctic TV programmes, not ideal for carrying anything on your back, although at least there were no polar bears, however with a struggle we made it.

This procedure went on for weeks and weeks, there would be falls of snow regularly, making it harder to get water out of the river, as with the build-up of the snow and sleet on top of the ice on the river, the ice got thicker and the water was getting lower, even the water inside the dwelling house would be frozen, and the milk as well. I would rarely light the fire or have anything to eat before I went out, the animals came first, this was my own choice. I was my own boss as far as these things were concerned or most things for that matter, but the work had to be done, I would feed all the outside cattle first, and by that time wee Tommy would have done most of the inside ones, but in the springtime the horses would come first, they needed to be fed early to be ready for a long hard days' work ahead of them, the horses and ourselves were always well fed despite the rationing.

Tom would always keep a pig for home curing and killing, he was class man at the job, and I don't suppose there are many, if anyone around now, who know how to cure a pig. We did not have Freezers in those days, at that time big stores would have what was called cold storage. It was like a building under the ground, it had air tight doors, apart from that, I don't know much about it.

I used to watch the curing process being done by Toms brother Willie, he would put lots of salt into the bacon, and also something called saltpetre, then wrap a clean cloth around the cut, and then put it into a large box, leaving about an inch of space between the sides and bottom of the box and the cut of meat. The same process was repeated until all the cuts were done, then on top of all the cuts, he put some very heavy weights, something like fifty six pound weights, these were used squeeze out a substance, it was called brine in my part of the country. The box containing the bacon cuts was raised off the ground by putting some timbers about three or four inches thick underneath the box, it would be left like that for some time, I can't remember exactly how long, then some of the weights would be taken off, and in a while some more, or maybe all of them, depending on if all the brine was squeezed out. When it was ready to eat, we would take enough of the wrapping off of enough meat to last maybe a week, then we would replace the wrapping on the rest of the cut. The piece to be used would be washed in clean cold water to wash the salt out of it. Sometimes a fairly large piece would be cut, and a hole made in it, a piece of string would be put through it, and it would be hung up near the chimney breast, at that time there would have been very big wide fire places in country houses, this gave the bacon a lovely smoky flavour, you could never buy any bacon as nice anywhere. I would have a fry nearly every morning, dip the bread in the gravy and maybe fry a few slices of bread as well, and never had a day's illness I would say to this day that it helped me to survive all the hard work and cold, I could have done with some of this in my childhood days when I needed it most.

That would last till late spring, but before then came Lent, this was supposed to be a time for prayer and penance, every Wednesday was a fast day and every Friday meat was forbidden, but it was allowed once on Saturdays. This all seemed unnecessary, every day was a fast day for lots of people, as they were lucky if they were able to afford meat once a week, but you could usually tell the protestant houses, by the smell of the meat cooking regularly. My boss Tom was a protestant, but he knew and remembered all the fast days better than me, sometimes I wished that he didn't, but he always ate the same as I was eating, he would not eat meat on a fast day. He probably would have made a better catholic than me, but many a time I said to myself, "I would have made a good protestant". Lent was a quiet time, there was no dances or card playing, I still used to go to the pictures, but my mother didn't know that.

CHAPTER 14

FOOTBALL AND SOCIAL EVENTS

We had no football team in our parish for a time, then a local lad Cahill "Frank" McKenna, (Frank was the family nickname, a lot of the McKenna's had nicknames, as there were a lot of them on the local townlands), anyway Cahill bought a football and everyone who wanted to play chipped in a few shillings, it was great idea it got a lot the local lads together, but we had no field of our own to play on, so we played anywhere that we saw an empty field. It was late autumn, and the fields would not be in use as much now, as they would earlier in the year. The first place we played was Peter Jemmy's meadow, I don't know if we had permission or not, but we played there for quite some time. We then moved across the road to John Nail's field, we had a bit more room there, nobody knew much about the right way to play, and it was mighty rough and dangerous stuff. Then after a winters break we moved to another field this time we did have permission, we named this, "Arbans meadow", it was quite a decent field compared to the others. All the people named above were nick names, and they were all McKennas, and we played there for quite some time, then in the spring we all got together and formed a club, and got it affiliated to the GAA. We formed a committee, some of them had never played football, and didn't know much about the game, but they were all, good, hard working, committee men. There were a few of the members of the old Clara Team on the committee as well, namely Joe "Lopen" McKenna, Arthur Finnegan and "Wishie" Finnegan. Then there were others of the committee who never played football at all. Just to mention a few, my brother Packie, James Treanor, Mick McKenna and Peter Oiney. Then there were other men who were not locals, namely Con Ahearn, he was a school teacher in Killybrone School, also Joe Collins who was a customs officer at Moybridge customs post, and also Tony Morgan, also a customs officer at Moybridge. Ahearn and Collins were both from county Cork, and Morgan was from county Roscommon, and they did great work for the club as well. We had some really good players, but we had nobody to train us properly. They were nearly all country lads, and they would be working very hard all day, and it would be late when we would get finished work, and the playing field was quite a bit away from most of the lads, and some might not even have a bike, I know I for one didn't have a bike. I rarely got to any practice at all, I didn't get a chance to play in many of the games for the first couple of years, but after a while I started to get some practise, and was then able to get my place on the team. Some of the older men that had played for the previous Clara team were too set in their ways, as to how the game should be played, and the game had changed a lot since their younger days. I remember one of the lads and myself were debating different methods of playing with one of the former players, it developed into quite a heated argument, and he was not impressed. We were told in no uncertain terms that we didn't know much about football. To a lot of the big hefty men on the previous Clara team, it was a catch and kick style, very little hand passing or short kicks, the point we were making was, maybe it would be better some times to play a low short kick to find someone out in an open space, and be able a provide a better chance to score, or to open up a chance to score, he said, "well that would suit you, because you rarely mark your man, and I have told you often enough, if he goes for a piss, you go with him", this was an expression some of the older boys used. We never managed to win any trophies, it was a pity because we had a lot of good players, the simple fact was that we did not have any sort of a system, and there were not many people around to give us the right advice. On the rare occasions that we had a few lads who were capable of showing us a better way of playing, unfortunately they were put off by the old diehards who resented other people interfering in their game, they would just shrug and say "what do they know about football."

At that time the clubs did not have much money to spare, their players had to buy their own boots and shorts, the club would only buy the jersey or shirt as it now called, a lot of materials were scarce, even after the war, lots of things were still on ration in the nineteen fifties, however we had a bit of luck with getting some of the materials. During the war all the houses north of the border had to have their windows blacked out, in case the Germans came over to drop bombs. There was a material which was used, it was a blackout blind, it was quite good material, there were lots of this stuff stored up, as nobody knew how long the war was going to last, the people who ran the stalls came from Belfast. One lady in particular everybody knew, was called Mrs McGibran, she was always very helpful and all her things were quite cheap, then there was a local woman, who was a good dressmaker, and she was able to make us shorts, or togs as they were called then, so we all wore McGibrans black togs.

At this time we also had a camogie team, and they were doing a lot better than the football team. I recall one fine Sunday afternoon we all headed off from Clara to travel to Ballygally on bikes, as hardly anyone had cars at this time, we went in the Ravella road into Aughnacloy, there must have been two hundred or more of us, there is a very steep hill up into Aughnacloy, so we had to get off our bikes and walk up the hill into the town, being a lovely day a lot of people were sitting outside their doors, it was hard to know what they were thinking, when they saw what looked like an army coming into their town, it looked an invasion from the South was taking place, I remember my cousin John Sherry saying he had never seen anything like it before or would ever be likely to see anything like it again. At this time the bike was the main means of travel, if you were lucky enough to have one, on occasions like this, we would hang our football boots on the handlebars of the bike, and stuff the togs inside one of the boots. We used to cycle to Clones to football matches, from Clara chapel to Clones is about 25 miles one way, one particular time was in the 1947, this was the year when the all-Ireland football final was being played in the Polo Grounds in New York, and the Ulster final was been played in Clones, which was the regular venue for the Ulster final. Monaghan had reached the semi-final in that year, the only team to hold Cavan to a draw, and were rather unlucky not to win the replay as well. Once Monaghan were out, we would always backed Cavan or whichever other Ulster team remained in the championship. So now it was Cavan vs Antrim in the Ulster final, which looked like being a great game, and everyone was looking forward to it, so once again it was a big turnout for the cyclists of Clara we all took off together, it was like the start of the Tour de France.

    I had borrowed a neighbour's bike, his name was Patrick "Boulway" McKenna, he lived just a short distance away, it was a lovely bike, and he was big tall man so he lowered the saddle to suit me. He gave me the bike the night before so I was well pleased, but when I got out on the road, I found out I could not get into top gear, some of the experts had a look at the bike, but no-one could figure out what was wrong. Jim O Hagan was a handy man with bikes, and even he could not figure out what wrong, so I had a tough ride to Clones. I could barely keep up with the rest, it didn't matter how fast I pedalled on the level road, I struggled to keep up with the rest of the group, I could gain a bit on hills, but we all managed to get there together. We parked our bikes, and walked up to the park, it had just started rain, and as we looked at the clock on the church tower, it was twelve o'clock, the minor game didn't start until two o'clock, and the rain was coming down in sheets and blowing a gale as well. We didn't have any waterproof then, and we just wanted to get a good side-line seat right on the touch line and as near to the centre of the pitch as possible. I didn't have to worry about top gear anymore, so I made sure I got where I wanted to be, right in the centre just beside where the teams came out. It rained throughout both games, it was hard to play good football in weather like that, with the wind behind them Cavan built up a big lead in the first half, they led by eleven points in as many minutes, Antrim managed to reduce the lead down to four points. Cavan seemed to have lifted their foot off the pedal in the second half, this was a powerful Cavan team. They went on to beat Roscommon in the all-Ireland semi-final by four points, and went on to beat Kerry in New York by four points. In those days, only the all-Ireland semi-finals and all-Ireland final would be broadcast, a lot people didn't have radios, some of my friends and I went to my cousins to hear it, there was some problem with the broadcasting company, and we were been told that we might not able to hear all of the game. I remember Michael O'Hehir was the commentator, he kept saying, give me five minutes more, this was the name of a popular song at the time, so we managed hear all of the match after all.

This was a good time for football every youngster was trying to imitate the big stars, even our own Clara team started to play better, but we only lasted a couple of more years, and as I said we didn't win any trophies, but we finished the season of nineteen forty eight quite well. I just don't know what went on behind the scenes, in the spring of forty nine a discussion was going on between the officials and committees of Clara and Emyvale, including Carrickroe, Ballyoisen and Mullan Mill, but none of the last three places mentioned had a football team at this time. I think the idea was to pick the best players from all the areas mentioned, it was supposed to be like some kind of parish league, so a number of teams formed and were given different names, like St Vincent's, which was the name of the team which I was selected to play for. There were about six teams all together, this was supposed to be a friendly affair, but it was far from it, everyone was trying to make a name for themselves, the Tournament was never finished, but the selection committee still selected names of players who gave a good performance, with the intention of forming one good team, nobody seemed to know what the team would be called. Some of us went to where the selectors were, hoping to see some of the names that were being selected, Peter Sherry was known as Peter of Cavan, everyone seemed to agree that they had heard Jimmy Sherry's name being mentioned, there was a bit of discussion, then I heard someone say I would never have him on my team, I had just played the best game I ever played, I scored two goals and three points. One of the other selectors said to him "he scored two goals and three points, so why wouldn't you have him in your team", his reply was there was nobody making him, anyway it all fell through, and our Clara team ceased to exist. There was no new team picked, and nobody seemed to know what went wrong, everyone just lost interest, some of lads went off and played for other clubs, I didn't really bother anymore, I had plenty of other interests.

I always wanted to learn to play an accordion myself, I mentioned earlier that I that learned to play the mouth organ and a few tunes on a little old melodeon that belonged to my friend and work mate Tommy O'Neill, better known as wee Tommy, so I was always on the lookout for a second hand accordion. I happened to mention it to my pal and neighbour Packie McKenna. Peter Jemmy was working for a man called Richard Falls, who had an accordion, and he was thinking of selling it, Packie said he would he ask him how much he wanted for it, and he wanted seven pounds for it. Packie arranged a night for me to go out to the man's house to have look it, seven pound doesn't seem a lot of money now, but in 1947 it was a hell of a lot of money to me, all my wages went to my mother, I never could have raised that kind of money, but I had a good run at the hunting, every place was covered with snow and ice, so the rabbits would have to come into the open to look for food. Rabbits and wild fowl were a great price at this time, I would leave a sheave of corn out, and it would not be long before something would arrive, and I would be lying under cover with a double barrel shotgun and plenty of ammunition. Although I hardly made a dent in the local population of rabbits, still I managed to raise enough money to buy the accordion. It needed some repairs to be done to it as well which were quite expensive, but it all turned out quite well in the end. I learned quite a lot of tunes, all the dances we were learning had a special tune for it, and knew all the tunes by ear by listing to Eugene Monaghan. Then Eugene asked me to bring the accordion in one night so he could have a tune on it, so I brought it the next week, and he played it the whole night He was very helpful to me, he had told me where to take the accordion to have it repaired, otherwise I would not have had a clue, at the end of that night, he said to me, "why don't you do the playing instead of me", I said "Eugene, you must be joking, me play here on my own", it frightened the life out of me, then he said bring your own accordion next week, and I will play a few tunes at the beginning of the might, and then you can have a go, and see how you feel about it, so I did what he told me to do, and it worked out better than I thought it would. I was really nervous playing in front of Eugene, but he was a very modest man, a real gentleman he could make you feel comfortable, he could, and has played with the best, at the end of that night he said they don't need me here anymore, you can do the job fine. I never had that kind of expectations, I felt bad about it, he was giving his job to me, I said, "Eugene you can't do this, you're losing a good nights pay, and I don't think it's fair", he said, "don't you worry about that, I have to cycle about six miles each way come hail, wind, or snow, and sometimes I don't feel like it", he said "give it a go and see how you get on". I did just that, and everything went well, sometimes there might come somebody else in and play a few tunes, and maybe be a worse player than me, it all helped to give me a little boost. Then as spring came around the dancers would be getting ready for the "feis", sometimes I might be asked to play a couple of nights a week extra, I got paid fifteen shilling per night, to me this was a fortune, there were some people only earning that much for a week's work.

But I had to look after the few shillings, the dancing classes ended in spring, and the hunting of the rabbits and wild fowl ended at the beginning of the month of march, so that ended the main cash flow, so I would be on the lookout for some who might want a hand to take something over the border, and earn a few shillings that way, as the hunting season didn't start again until the end of September. But I got a lot of fun out of it all, I got invites to house parties, there was always something to look forward to, and there was a great bunch of lads about at the time, they would go about in little groups, the McKenna's, Peter Jemmie's brothers, who lived just across the field, and myself and my brothers would pal about together. We never had any arguments amongst ourselves, and we always backed each other if there were any trouble from outside neighbourhoods. Sometimes they would come up to our house on a Sunday afternoon or a Sunday night for a game of cards, if there was nothing else going on, but it now reached a point, that there were so many things going on it was hard to fit them all in. My brother Felix had just joined the Glaslough Harriers, he asked me if I would like to join, and I said I would try it out, we trained every Sunday afternoon at Glaslough, so that ended the Sunday afternoon card playing for me. I won't dwell too much on the Glaslough Harriers, their history has already been well written. I always loved music, but I always hoped that someday that I would like to play in a marching band. Nearly all the Catholic marching bands in Ulster were funded and ran by the Ancient Order of Hibernians, they were a non-political organization, and although the stipulation was that you had to be a Roman Catholic.

So at an early age I joined the Aughnacloy AOH, my brothers Peter and Packie were already members, also my cousin John Sherry was a member, there were quite a good number of members in the Division, all the groups of the AOH were known as Divisions, and each Division had a number, you would be given a password, which would be changed and renewed once a month. Some Divisions had their own Clubs, if you were away from home, in some other town, if you found their Club you could knock, give the password and get in and have a drink.

They Ancient Order of Hibernians is indeed what it says, very Ancient, the Yanks have tried to claim it, and some Scottish people think its theirs, but it was founded in Ireland hundreds of years ago to help the poor. They were not a rich organization, the members paid in a small subscription every month, we would run dances in the hall about once a month, and sometimes rented it out for other social events, it all helped to raise funds. We would find out from time to time if there was some elderly person who might need a bit of help, and give them something, like a bag of coal or a little flour, and try and not let anyone know about it. The AOH and The Nationalist party were one of the same, the AOH organized the two big parades, St Patrick's Day and the 15th August. They had a lot of experience in organizing parades, every county had their own county board, and they decided in which town or place the parades would be held. Some places didn't want the responsibility of holding the parades, it was a lot of hard work, as we were to find out later on. When I was just a young boy, I used to look forward to these two days, Aughnacloy AOH did not have a band of their own, they would hire a band for the day, my brother Felix and myself would be holding the banner strings. There were four strings on the banner, two at the front, and two at the back, these were used to stabilize the banner. The two men who would be carrying the banner would have a harness round their shoulders, each of these had a socket, in which the end of the banner poles would be placed into. The banners were quite big and could be quite hard work on a windy day, this is where the boys on the banner strings came in handy, if there was a strong wind blowing, the boys on the strings would have to keep their minds on the job, by keeping strings tight or slack according to how the wind was blowing, my brother Felix and I had done it so many times we had it down to a fine art.

After a while some of our members began to raise the question, why none of the parades had been held in Aughnacloy over a long number of years, after all Aughnacloy had a big wide long street, in fact the widest street in Northern Ireland, and should be an ideal place to hold a parade. Some of the older members who had more experience than us younger members, while they were not against applying to have the parade held in Aughnacloy, they had the experience of the hard work and worry it would cause. They knew what it was all about because they had done it before, however we all agreed and decided to apply to have a Saint Patrick's parade to be held in Aughnacloy, it was 17th March 1950. The decision making would be done at the Tyrone County Board of the AOH, and it was agreed it would be held in Aughnacloy. My brother Packie and James O'Neill were the two delegates who attended the meeting, another big decision was made at that meeting, two tricolours would be carried in front of the Parade, this had never happened before at any of the parades in Northern Ireland, little we knew when we applied for the parade to be held in Aughnacloy the impact it was going to have on that part of the country and beyond.

    My brother Packie and James O Neill had arranged with some people they met in Fivemiletown, who said they could get all the buntings that we would need, and arrange to have them sent over on the Ulster transport bus to Lambs bus depot, where it could be collected by us. They were to send them a few days before the parade, in those days there were not many who had cars, and fewer people had telephones, so it was not easy to get in touch with anybody. My brother Packie, James O Neill and myself met in Aughnacloy on the 16th at about seven o'clock in the evening, we waited as long we could at Lambs hoping the buntings would arrive, but nothing arrived, and no news from any one about them. So now we had a big problem, it was eight o'clock and time was running out fast, and all the fuss we had made about getting the parade held in Aughnacloy, we were going to be a right laughing stock. We had to think hard and fast, we went to my cousin John Sherry's house, where we sat down in the warm and talked it over, we came up with a few ideas, we decided we would try and buy some white calico cloth to try and make the bunting, we would need about ninety yards, but how or where were we going to get it, every place was closed. We also needed enough rope to reach three times across Aughnacloy's main street, and as I said the street was the widest main street in Northern Ireland. We also needed a lot of sewing machine thread, as there was a lot sewing and hemming to be done. The first thing we needed to do was to find out if all these materials were available. The first place we went to was Daly's drapers shop, and they were able to give us all the cloth we wanted, once we had explained our position to them. We said we would check out the other materials, to make sure they were available, before we could buy the cloth. So we had to check everything out before we bought anything, the smallest items took up more of our time to get sorted out than the largest ones. The smallest item was the dye, finding enough of the right colours we needed took a lot of our time, we had to go to three different shops to find the orange and green dye's, we eventually got them from Frank Quinns Hardware shop, and collected all our other items, and we were ready to put our plan into operation. Our plan was to cut the cloth into three lengths, each thirty yards long, and about four feet wide. The roll of cloth we bought was a hundred yards long, the extra few yards would allow for any mistakes. Our plan was to dye two sections of each length, one length green, and the other orange, leaving the white in-between. Now this was not going to be an easy task, but we were lucky a local man offered to help, and we were grateful for his help, without it, it would have been almost impossible to do what we had in mind. He was a painter and decorator by trade, he had a set of extension ladders, which was just what we needed, then through him we got use of his brothers and sisters house, which was the house where he used live himself. His name was Packie McKenna, he was better known as Packie Dunn, that was the family nickname, he had a sister Ellen and two brothers James and Francis, Francis was better known as Andy, unfortunately Andy was in poor health at this time otherwise he would have been right in the middle of it all. Their uncle Jimmy Cush had been a member of the Aughnacloy AOH, so the family were always willing helpers, sometimes Packie would get a bit carried away, but he was a great help to us, one of the most vital members of our team was Packies sister Ellen, as she was a dress maker, and whilst the lads were great hard workers, and keen to help, we had very poor needlework skills.

Ellen got three lengths of cloth cut and the dye ready for use, now this may sound like fiction, but it was truly like the A team in action. McKenna's house was in Ravella Road, and my Cousin John Sherry's was just across the road, at that time this road was known as Truagh Lane. Ellen got started with the dyeing of the lengths of cloth, when the first was done, we took it across to John Sherry's house and put it the oven of the stove to dry, we called these stoves ranges, today the popular name outside of Ireland would be an Aga. In the meantime Ellen was dyeing the next section, and when it was dyed, it was put in the oven of their own house, and so on until all the lengths were dyed. As it was impossible to dye the cloth in a straight line, Ellen had to fold the cloth and hem it, to make look as if came out of a factory, she did a fantastic job. Then she had to hem top of the cloth, leaving a hole to tread the rope through to suspend the banner, this was another time consuming job. At the same time myself and another fellow were out along the street, trying to find a suitable house to tie the buntings to, some of the houses or shops were not too keen on having anything like that fixed to their house or shop, even if they were on the same way of thinking as us, they didn't want to offend their neighbours, especially the shops, it might not do their business any good.

I have generally given the impression throughout this book that relations between catholic and protestant communities was quite good, and generally it was, but that did not mean that there were not bad minded people about.

Anyway we found a house near the top of Moor street, and a lamp post on the other side of the street which we could tie on to, the next banner was secured to Annie B. Gillmartin's public house, she had freely given us permission, and we tied the other end of this bunting to in the bell tower of market house, whilst fixing this one, we disturbed a flock pigeons, and the flapping of their wings made a noise like a burst of machine gun fire, we thought we were going to wake the whole town up. The third and last one was hung from Daly's drapers shop on one side of the street across to "Earlys" shop. Now our last job was to put a tricolour on the AOH hall, and there was a socket already fixed for the purpose, all we had to do hoist the flag into socket and the job was finished. We were well pleased with ourselves, we caused no trouble, or disturbed any ones sleep, whilst hanging our three buntings, or flags, or whatever you liked to call them. Now they were fluttering nicely in the wind it was now around six o'clock in the morning, now it was time for home, and try and get a bit of a rest. The residents of Aughnacloy must have been very surprised when they looked out that morning and saw what went on during the night, I am sure quite a few were shocked, I look back and think this was done by just five people, and I must say that Ellen played a big part in it, we certainly could not have done the job without her, she had as the saying goes, a great pair of hands. We all went home, got washed, and had a bit to eat. I didn't go to bed at all, I might have dozed for a short while on the chair, and I was too fired up to sleep. Anyway, we arranged to meet in the town around ten in the morning, to finish off whatever was needed to be done, we were hoping that there would be a big turnout, bands were supposed to be arriving quite early. I was in the town in time to go to nine o'clock Mass, the rest of the team turned up in good time as well. The bands that were coming to take part in the parade starting to arrive around twelve noon, we needed to be there to make sure everybody knew their positions, and to organise the order of the bands.

Aughnacloy Riots.

The parade was to start from over the top of Moor Street, just in front of where the Supermarket is now, the bands were coming in from the Dungannon, Caledon or Monaghan roads, would parade up the main street, and out to the junction of the Ballygally and Augher road, where there was, and still is, a little piece of ground, a sort of three corner shaped piece of ground with a wall built around it, at that time it was called finger post, the bands would go around there, and up to where the parade was to start from.

It had been agreed at the Tyrone County Board of AOH, that two Tricolours would carried in front of the parade, and our division of Aughnacloy, being the host, it was custom to lead the parade. My cousin John Sherry was one of the men selected to carry one of the flags, and a man by the name of McKearney from Fivemiletown was selected to carry the other flag. Each bearer was to have someone walking alongside them, in case any trouble makers would try and grab the flags, I would walk alongside John, and James O'Neill alongside the other man. But before we got started, we had some problems with the RUC, the DI said we could only show two colours green and white, that we would not be allowed to show the orange, I tried to explain to him that the orange in the flag represents, equally the orange men an all other non-Catholics, with the white for purity between the green and orange. But that's as far as we got on the subject, the crowd started pushing forward and shouting to roll out the flags and let them fly, the bands struck up the music and we were on our way, the police sensed there would be trouble if they continued interfering and moved back, it was a wise thing to do, We didn't want trouble of any kind, we wanted everything to off peacefully, it was the first time the Tricolour was ever carried in Aughnacloy or as far as I know in any other part of Northern Ireland. The AOH always organized and ran the St Patrick's day parades, also the Fifteenth of August, I always went to all the those parades since I was a boy, and I had never seen a Tricolour being carried in front of any of the parades. The tricolour flag was only given constitutional status in 1937, and had been initially adopted at the time of the 1916 Easter rising, so this explains why the flag had not been flown in Northern Ireland before. The reason John Sherry was selected by our Division to carry the flag, was because he was a very quiet inoffensive man, and well-liked by everyone, and the other flag bearer was like wise. We marched down the main street and around the little triangular island, and up again to where the platform and the speakers were, just beside the market house. When the speaking was over, we marched down to the Hibernian Hall, put the banner in the hall, we could not fold it properly because it was wet, we just stood it up against the wall. We went back up the town well pleased with ourselves, how well everything went without any trouble. We were meeting people, they were congratulating us on the great job we had done. But sometime later a few of us were making our way down the main street again, we could see a lot people gathered in the lower part of the town, as we got further down the town we could see someone carrying a tricolour, when we got a bit closer we could see it was Packie "Dunn" McKenna, he was waving it about, and getting close to the RUC barracks. Then we knew there was going to be trouble, when he got down as far as the barracks he stopped and waved the flag in front of the barracks. Suddenly from the front of the barracks came a crowd of police, all hell broke loose, there were batons flying in all directions, there was blood running down Packie Dunns face, the Police were sort of dragging and half carrying him towards the barracks, and swinging batons at any one who was within reach of them. At that time there were a lot of the parts of the footpaths made up with round paving stones, just down a bit from the barracks near a big house, which then belonged to Jim Rea the solicitor, the crowd started prising them out of the ground, and began pelting the police with them, at this time, some bands would have someone walking in front of the band carrying what they called a pike, now this is not to be confused with the mace, which a lot of bands still carry today. This was more of an ornamental thing, it was it was about six feet long and a little thicker than a broom handle, it had a little brass ornamental thing on top of that looked like a spear, but the point was not sharp, it was round and blunt, but could be used quite effectively to prise stones out of the ground, this gave the crowd plenty of ammunition. One big Policeman seemed to be putting himself about a lot, he made his way to where the stones were been thrown from, and made an attempt to arrest someone, he got hit on the head with one of these pikes it knocked him out, as he fell he rolled off the footpath into a water channel, which was a bit deeper than normal, usually the channel would drain the rain water away, but it had been pelting rain, he was blocking the channel, so the water was running over him. Then a group of police came to try rescue him, they tried to take him back into the barracks, but they could not manage it, Jim Rea's house was just a few yards from where the policeman was lying, so they grabbed him and took him into Rea's house. When the crowd gathered around seen this they started smashing the windows of Rea's house. Fortunately then the crowd was drawn towards the other end of the town by someone in the middle of the crowd waving the flag, but the police did not try to intervene so the crowd dispersed into pubs and houses.

But our day was not over yet, I had keep my wits about me, as we were told by the Police that all the buntings and flags were to be taken down by midnight so I could not enjoy myself yet, we had to get our little team together again and one was in the Police Barracks, like I said earlier Packie Dunn would get a bit carried away sometimes. I found a good replacement, a good able man, he was our neighbour, Francis "Nail" Mc Kenna, and he used to come out to a lot of parades with us. We got started early and managed to get all our buntings and flags down, everything was left in Dunn's that night, but I don't know what ever happened to them all, but I would have liked to have had something as a keepsake. It was certainly a day to remember in the history of Aughnacloy, I always enjoyed all the parades from I was a young boy, but this was one I did not enjoy.

The other sad thing about this day, my cousin John Sherry never came back to the Hibernians after that day, nor did my brother Packie, is was a loss to the division because, John was an excellent secretary and would have a very steadying effect on everything, and my brother Packie was a great organizer, they were both badly missed.

Getting back to the history of the parades, we carried on as usual the following year, we would hire a band to come with us on the day of the parades, most of the time it would be the Davagh flute band, Davagh was only a short distance away from Aughnacloy, and we knew all the lads in the band which was better for everyone. This band was also organized and ran by the Davagh Hibernians. When we would get back home from the parade in the evening, we would have a few drinks, and there would be a few heated debates, mainly from the older members. They would maintain that they were the true Hibernians and that we were Republicans, we always classed ourselves as staunch Nationalists, and we promoted the Nationalist cause throughout Ulster for years. We had our debates and disagreements but we never fell out, it was mainly the older members who took part in the debates.

Then one day the Davagh band had a bit of a disagreement amongst themselves. We had hired them for a demonstration that was being held in a town called Newtownstewart in County Tyrone.

The disagreement was amongst some of the drummers, some of the lads were a bit late getting back to the bus that was taking us home from the parade, which was nothing unusual on these kind of days, but the disagreement was between them, we were the people that hired them, but we didn't want to get involved in their argument, it all got blown out of proportion. James O'Neill and I were trying to make sure that there was nobody left behind. The older members of our Division were very angry about what happened, and they vowed they would never have that band with us again. Anyway James O'Neill and I were sitting on a seat by ourselves, and the very same words were about to come out of both our mouths at the same time, only and I managed to say it first, "we will have our own band for St Patrick day", and James said, "you took the words right out of my mouth".

Many years later I met a man in England, he asked me where I came from, I said Monaghan, he said he took me for a Tyrone man, I said I lived and worked in Tyrone for years, he asked, "whereabouts in Tyrone", and I told him about a mile from a little town called Aughnacloy, he asked me if I was there on the day of the riots, I said, "I was part of what caused those riots"

I told him the whole story of how I was involved in helping to organize the parade, and what caused the riots to start, when I mentioned about the policeman lying in the water channel and the water running over him, he looked at me for a few seconds and said, "hold on a minute I was right there beside him!". We could have rubbed shoulders or spoken to one another, there was no mistake in what he said, he described the big red house where they took the policeman into, and the crowds smashing the windows. He told me that he got the bamboo pole of one of the flags, and as far as he knew some of his family in Ireland still have it, then I said, "here's another surprise, my brother has part of the policeman's helmet, the crowd had been kicking it about and my brother got hold of it, the peak was missing, but had he rolled it up and put it in his pocket, and to the best of my knowledge it's still in the house at home in Ireland". It's hard to believe that we met after all those years, he told me the reason he was there was, that the parade that he would have been going to on that day had been banned, it was to be held in a town called Dunloy in County Antrim, so that meant most of the crowd that would have been there came to Aughnacloy and swelled our ranks!

This man's name was Hugh O'Neill, it was strange because I had known him for quite some time and he never got around to asking me before where I was from. He used to come into the old Irish club in Brompton, he was a great singer of any kind of songs, but his favourites were Irish rebel songs, he used to take his son Dean with him, and Dean would sit watching me playing the drums on the stage, then one night Hugh asked me if I would let his son have a go on the drums. I said of course I will, I had a nice little stool which could be adjusted to suit people of different heights, I got it about right for him, he had been having some drum lessons at the time, and he did really well. Honestly up until that time I didn't know he was having lessons. After sometime his Father bought him a nice small set which he would take into the club nearly every Saturday night, I would leave my set to one side and let him have a go for a while. Everything went great then, poor Hugh's marriage failed. I think he never got over it really, he kept coming to the club for a while, and then he stopped coming for a long time. The young lad was beginning grow up now and I didn't see him for years. When I met Hugh again sometime later, he told me that Dean had joined a band and was playing over in Holland most of the time. But Hugh was never the same man again, after the breakup he never sang again he was a lovely man, he never drank, nor smoked, he used to say he didn't need either

CHAPTER 15

A DREAM COME TRUE

As a young lad I always dreamed about having our own local marching band, but at that time, it was nearly all flute and bagpipe, and the odd brass band that dominated the scene. It was only latter that accordion bands appeared on the scene. The Davagh flute and drum band was always there as long as I could remember, we also had a flute and drum band in Clara but I never seen or heard it, I used to hear a lot about it from my cousin Peter who was a drummer in it, as I mentioned earlier I was living with Peters family as a child at that time.

Now this is the time to make my dream come true, it was "James' Dream". We decided we bring it up at the next monthly meeting of the AOH, which was always held on the first Sunday of the month, our first meeting would be on the first Sunday of September. I said to James that I would propose that we would like to try and start our own band, if he would like to second it, or the other round if he wished. We didn't think this was going to be easy, we had a good bit of groundwork to be done here, we needed to get the older members wound up a bit, and let them vent their anger and disgust, so as we might have an easier passage, and they did just that. Then after things had calmed down a bit, I thought this is the right time to put forward my proposition that we should try and start our own band in

Aughnacloy, provided it could be funded by the Aughnacloy AOH Division. There was a long, although sensible discussion about it, some of the older members had some doubts whether we could do it or not, but there was not a word of anger or disagreement about the proposal. I had said that I would like to see a unanimous decision, James O Neill seconded my proposal and it was carried unanimously, it was just unbelievable. James and I were on cloud nine, and so was everyone else, we were not a rich organization, we did not have a big bank balance, we raised our funds running dances quite regularly, and from the monthly subscriptions from members. It was agreed that the money could be withdrawn as soon as possible, the accordions were quite expensive, we decided to buy a small number of accordions just to get started, and we were given a bass drum or what was always called the big drum. It had belonged to an old Clara band, and there were some of the members of that band still around, and they said we could have it. Very soon we got the accordions and started to practise, there were only a few of us who could play well, and then there were a few who could sort of play a little bit. So those of us who could play, helped the others along, there were not many teachers of accordions around at that time, that's the way it was at that time, most people were self-taught, you had to have an ear for music, and then with a little help they would soon pick it up, and it wasn't until we were beginning to blend together that it all started to become more and more exciting.

Our aim was to be ready for St Patrick's Day, but we needed drummers, and we didn't have any, except my cousin Peter Sherry, and we needed him for the big drum. We found a teacher for the drummers, his name was Peter Treanor, he was the leading drummer with the Davagh band, and also with Monaghan brass band he had years of experience as a drummer.

We arranged to have our first practice, it was held in Ivy hill, this was initially to be only temporary, as this was supposed to be an Aughnacloy band, and that was supposed to be where its headquarters should be. Some of the members were unhappy about this, I think Ivy Hill was the ideal place to get started, there were plenty of spare rooms, so different things could be going at the same time, you could have little groups who were a little bit behind with their learning getting a little bit of extra attention where it was less noisy. Everything was going so well, some were beginning to think, maybe we could be ready to play at mid night mass in Clara.

It was now mid-October and still a lot to do, we had no drummers ready yet, but we soon got the drumming lessons started, it was quite a slow process, it was just as well we had plenty of spare rooms, the drummers had their own separate room, and it was one noisy place, but there was not a drum in sight. There was a big long wooden table in the middle of the floor, with the teacher on one side, and the pupils on the other side, this was how and where they learned to play the drum. It would take a very long time to find out who was going to make the drummers, and some would give up after a short time.

Wishie Finnegan was the man who kindly let us practise in his house, he had his mind set to be ready and able to play at midnight mass in Clara. Now Wishie was a hard man to hold back, and some of us had doubts about this, what we didn't want was to go there not prepared well enough and make fools of ourselves. We decided to keep the proposed plan quiet, and see how we would get on. Everyone was making every effort to make it happen, the lads who were learning to drum would certainly not be ready, but we were able to solve that problem, Peter Treanor the man who was teaching the drummers, would play the kettle drum, and my cousin, big Peter, as he became better known, and would beat the big drum. We had eight new accordions and we had eight boys who could play, there were some weak ones, but they still had time to improve, we all had a good bit to do, like learning to march, play and keep in step, always starting with the roll of the drum on the left foot, and finish off with the roll of the drum on the left foot. The man on the big drum would give the signal with a double tap on the big drum, he might do this two or three times to make sure everyone heard it. These things were very important, and if you did go out of step, there was a quick little skip you would give to get back in step again, it was a good thing to practice. Of course my brother Felix and myself were well used to marching with bands on the big parades, we were always holding the banner strings.

By now a lot of the hard work had been done, we had been marching round the room every practice night, now we thought it was time to give it a try out on the road. The weather would not always be in our favour, at last we found a suitable night and out we went. We marched up as far as Errigal crossroads and turned around and marched back again, it's about 2 miles in each direction, it went quite well. It was a lot different from being inside, the volume was a lot lower, but there were no big problems, and there was not the traffic on the roads in those days, we still wanted to keep as quiet as possible, in case anything happened that we couldn't turn out, we were all getting excited about it all, we were counting the days to Christmas and hoping the weather would be good.

Then we began to think, maybe we should have some kind of light in front of the band, Wishie Finnegan came up an idea, he had a piece of plywood and he cut it in the shape of a cross, then drilled some holes in it. We got some battery lamp bulbs which we inserted into the holes, then attached a twin cell battery with some kind of a switch, there were no DIY stores around that time, no quick or easy way of doing things. All this clever work was done by a man called Seamus Speer from Aughnacloy, he owned a bicycle repair shop, and sold some electric items as well as some other things. He was a bit of a handy man, anyway he got it all together for us, and when the lights were switched on it was like a little star. We arrived early at Ivy Hill, so we had a good run through all the tunes that we were going to play, we had hoped and prayed that the weather would be good, and our prayers were answered it was a lovely calm night. We had eight accordion players, three of us in the front row, myself, Wishie Finnegan and James O'Neill, in the second row was my brother Arthur and Kevin Maguire, and the third row, Kevin "Larry" Mc Kenna and his brother Vincent, in the fourth row, Peter Treanor, drummer, and big Peter Sherry, big drummer, and James Traynor on accordion, I can't recall who carried the light in front.

We marched from Ivy Hill to Clara Church, we started off good and early, which give us plenty of time to play a good few hymns outside the church before mass started, strange as it may seem, but a lot of people didn't know of our existence, considering that nearly everything that went on in the townland would be well known about, even sometimes nearly before it happened. We got a great reception from everyone, we played some more outside church after mass, and then we played all the way back to Ivy Hill. There was lots of food and drinks ready for us, it was a night to remember, and it was the first of many good outings which lay ahead of us.

Now we had to begin in earnest, it was only about six weeks to St Patrick's day, and we had a lot of work to do, we needed at least two drummers ready, my brother Felix and Al Stone were practicing hard on the drumming, we bought eight more new accordions, but we only managed to get four recruits to learn to play them, they were, Mick Rafferty, Felix McCarron Junior, Peter Sweeny and Francis MacMullin, some of them could play a bit, but needed knocking into shape. We were a bit disappointed that we didn't people to play all the accordions, but the main thing now was to get everyone drilled, and up to scratch. We added another man to march in front of the band to carry the mace. His name was Joe Woods, a long-time and dear friend of mine.

The next thing we needed was a uniform of some kind, we had a long discussion about it, and we decided we would have black trousers and white shirts, with a black dickey bowtie, and get some plaid cloth made up in the shape of a cloak, or shawl, with two straps tied at the shoulders, crossed over the chest and tied at the sides, and we wore a "Glengarry" cap made from the same cloth as the cloak, it was like a tartan design, it looked great and it was original. We were the envy of the other bands at the demonstration that was held in Dungannon. We marched from the Hibernian hall in Aughnacloy up to the top of the town, turned around at the Catholic Church, and marched back down to the hall again. We got a great reception, there were lots of people lined along the street, it was a day to be proud of, after all the hard work and planning we put into it, we boarded our buses outside the hall and off we went to Dungannon.

Now most of the lads would not have had any experience of marching in parades like this. Sometimes there might be thirty or forty bands taking part in the parade. There would be bagpipe bands, flute, brass and accordion bands. Dungannon was quite a big town but like most towns the streets were narrow, you would be marching through a narrow street with bands in front of you and bands behind you, and you might be meeting bands coming down the street towards you, there were some streets we would not be allowed to go through, such Church street or Scotch street, it was the same situation with the orange bands on the 12th July, they were not allowed to go through Irish or Scottish streets, we were blessed once again with lovely weather, there was a great turn out of bands, we had a great day, we paraded up and down Aughnacloy's main street when we got home, and stopped at the diamond, and played lots of tunes, it was just great to be part of it all, we were in great demand all through the summer months at gatherings of all sorts.

Going to "An Tohscal" was a big test for my brother Felix, as it was his first to be the lead drummer, and everything depended on him getting it right, but he came through with flying colours.

The two most outstanding events took place the following year, the first one was taking part in the big parade through Dublin in 1953, "An Tohscal". It certainly was an unforgettable day for all kind of reasons. We all had a really terrific day, Joe Woods and I were always good pals, and we broke off on our own to do our thing. We thought we might as well live up like the rich for one day, so we picked a first class hotel, it was the royal Hibernian hotel. They sat us down at a table and took our coats, then they came around with the menu and asked what we would like, Joe says, "the best you have got!" They recommended the sirloin steak, we said we'll have that and all the trimmings, then they asked if we would like something to drink, and we said we would have a large brandy each. I don't know how we managed to pay for it, but we did, with something to spare, and we were not finished yet. We asked if there was comfortable bar where we could have a drink, the waiter showed us to a bar upstairs, and there we met a business man from Aughnacloy having a quiet drink by himself, I am sure we were the last two people he expected to see, but he was a real gentleman at home or away, after some time he sent two large brandy's to our table. After a while he came over and sat down and talked to us, he said he would appreciate it if we didn't mention to anyone that we had seen him here, and we said that we would not mention it to anyone, and we never did, and I won't be breaking that promise now. When we were leaving we went back down stairs to get our coats, they came back with these two lovely black overcoats, but they were not ours, but the staff insisted that they were ours, and that they were the only ones left, but we insisted that the were not ours. What a pair of fools we were, the overcoats just looked right for the way we were dressed, but we were just too honest, and I suppose we would have a lot of explaining to do to our mothers, if we arrived home with better coats than we went away.

Then we headed for the Mansion House, Mary O'Hara was there playing the harp and singing, and other different performers as well. There was a big Ceili being held there, it was a great night of music singing and dancing, but as with all good things, it had to come to an end.

We had to make our way to the bus and face the long journey home. It was a real bitter cold frosty night, the bus was like a freezer and it was not functioning very well, it took us eight hours to get home, I never felt so cold in my life, we had been in the heat all night and had quite a few drinks, I suppose it was all beginning to take its toll, but it was all worthwhile.

The next big occasion was to play at the opening of Casement Park in Belfast, of all the big days, this was the most memorable. It was very special to have the honour of being invited to such a big occasion, the Ulster Senior Football Final, Cavan vs Armagh, and it was our band which led the teams on to the Park and played the National Anthem.

It was a special occasion for my brother Felix, when Ulster runners carried a flame from the birthplace of the GAA in Thurles

James Sherry

to Casement Park for the official opening of the now famous venue, keeping two or three runners on the road throughout journey, Felix ran four or five legs of the journey, it commenced in Thurles on Saturday evening at 6 pm, arriving at Casement Park at 2 p.m. on the Sunday in time for the opening ceremony, this was a journey of 171 miles, they ran throughout the night accompanied by a van which provided rest and refreshments for the participants between their stints on the road.

We were all very proud to be part of such a big occasion this was the summer of 1953.

CHAPTER 16

GETTING A BIT RESTLESS

I THINK IF the marching band had not started when it did, I think I would have made a move and went off to England or America, one thing happened that almost made my mind up to go, our horse died. You could say I grew up with him, we had him from when he was a colt. I helped to train him he was just like a friend, I worked with him for ten years, and I felt very down. Then shortly after that our dog died, people might find all this hard to understand another good friend gone, and before that my friend and work mate left to go and live in Belfast, it had become a bit of a lonely place now.

Then another thing happened that changed my outlook on things quite a bit, and that was the formation of Aughnacloy GAA Club. A School Teacher called John Ritchie arrived in Aughnacloy to teach in St Mary's school, he was very keen to get a GAA Club started. There had not a club there for years, I certainly could not ever remember one being there, but that did not deter John Ritchie, he got together with Matt O'Brien, who was a great GAA supporter, together with Tommy Hughes and big Brendan Landers, also Paddy Kelly, and a few others, they were all great workers, but it was never going to be easy. At that time soccer had been gaining a lot of support around the town, and at that time, the GAA had restrictions on anyone belonging to the GAA, taking part or playing soccer, it was going to be hard enough to get players around Aughnacloy to form a team.

Lucky for everyone at that time there was no football team in Clara, but there were a good few lads about who could help to build a team, but most of them had not played for two or three years. I had not kicked a ball for three and half years. It was decided to hold a meeting in St Mary's School and make a start to get things moving, this was in 1952, and it was coming near the end of the football season, so we would not be taking part in any games until the season started again in 1953.

The meeting went well, there had been a lot of work going on behind the scenes looking for a playing field, Mrs McKenna of Ravella kindly let us have a field, it was always known as, "Peter Jacks hoop", the Blackwater ran around it in a sort of a hooped shape, the field was just beside Ravella bridge, all the lads got stuck in and got a good bit of training in before the winter. I was running with the Glaslough Harriers, and training had started for them as well. I would go to Glaslough with my brothers Felix and Arthur on Sundays, this was the day when the races would be run. I would then have to try and get back a bit early in the evening, to get a bit of training at the football, there was never much time to spare, and working on a farm was always hard work.

We were beginning to get ourselves into shape, we had a great body of men on the committee, men who knew what they were doing, and trying to get a team that knew what they were doing, we listened to their advice, and they listened to our ideas, we had a good playing field to play on, better than most of the other fields that we had to play against other teams on. But like all the other places which we played at, there were never any place to change, except behind a hedge, once changed we covered our cloths with an overcoat in case it rained, no luxurious dressing rooms in those days. But there was a great team spirit, they were a great bunch of lads, we were looking forward to the start of the season, our first game was against Moy. It was a home game and it was a knockout competition, and we were being told that they were a good side, probably the best team in our league, their best player was George McGuigan, he played midfield and he was the man to watch, so they decided to give me the job of keeping him quiet. He wasn't much taller than me, but heavier built, but I was faster on the ball, Frank Quinn was playing in midfield along with me, Frank was quite tall and we talked it over with Matt O'Brien, and his counterparts that Frank would break the ball down to me. During the match George and myself had some tussles and some eyeball to eyeball, and a bit of shoving but shook hands at the end, but with all our planning, they managed to beat us, but only by a few points. We had never played together as a team before, and some of the lads had never played in a full game before, so we felt that we gave fairly good account of ourselves.

Our first game over, but we hadn't seen anything yet, our next game was away from home at Windmill, they had quite a reputation, nobody ever wins there. We could see why as soon as we arrived there, there were men all along the side line with sticks in their hands, and they looked a bit young to be using them for walking sticks. It was really rough stuff on the field, most of the players were really big men, a lot bigger than any of us, one of them tried to take Frank out of the game, but Frank had himself balanced right, and the other fellow came off worse. I remember him picking himself up, turning to Frank and saying, "I was going to play the nice way, now you had better watch out", but that didn't bother Frank too much, they used to say, it's when they don't warn you, they are more likely to come after you.

So far, so good, we were holding our own with them, we were a point behind them, the ball came across towards me, I was close to the side-line, as I went for the ball, I saw a man come running towards me with a stick in his hand, so I suppose I panicked a bit and tried to kick off with my left foot, which was my weaker foot, I didn't think I hit it very well, so I ran after it as it was bobbling along on the ground, I was hoping to catch up with it and stick it in the net, the goalkeeper was watching me going towards him, it bounced, hit the inside of the upright, and over the line for a goal, which put us a point in front of them. There were only a few minutes left, but it seemed to last forever before the final whistle went, in the meantime, Matt O Brian had told the captain Frank Quinn to spread word to all the players, to go straight to the bus as soon as the whistle goes, and not worry about our clothes, they had already gotten them back safely onto the bus. There was a crowd gathered around the bus when we got into, it shouting and shaking the bus, it didn't bother us too much anyway.

We would always get the report of all the matches in the Dungannon Observer, we would meet quite often in Matt O'Brien's, Matt was a shoemaker he worked very long hours, maybe up until midnight sometimes, he would work and talk away at the same time, many a match was replayed in that shop, on the Friday evening after the Windmill match, there were a few of the lads in there. When John Ritchie came in with the newspaper he was fuming, he said, "will you look at this, they have put our game with Windmill down as a draw, we won the match by a point". He went to Observer office the next day, only to be told that that was the report they got, and they were only publishing the result that they got from the referee. What happened, was that after the match the Windmill players got hold of the referee, and made him change the result to a draw, it was made to look as if there was some kind of mistake between the referee and our officials, so the game had to be replayed, but this time at home, it was a really dirty niggly match, which we could, and should have won, I got pulled down inside the square got a penalty. I never took penalties, Paddy Brady always took them, but this time the keeper saved it.

But there was a bit more drama yet to come. There was a local man at the match, who at this time was living in Magherafelt, County Derry, and he recognized two of the players that Windmill had playing for them, the both were players belonging to a team in County Derry. We brought the matter to the Tyrone County Board, we won our case, and the match was awarded to us. The two players and the Windmill club were suspended. Ordinarily there is no way I would want to win like that, but they did not win it right in the first place.

Then later on in the year we had more drama, we were playing in a tournament at a place called Galbly. There were six teams in the competition, they were all hard tough games, we won through to the final against Galbly, it was a real tough hard game, do or die stuff, again I was the one to be brought down inside the square, it was more like a rugby tackle, he rolled me over the line out of the square, and tried to convince the referee that it happened outside the square, but the referee knew better and gave a penalty, this time Paddy Brady didn't miss. After we scored, one of their players grabbed the referee by the throat, and all hell broke loose. He was one of the best referees around, he managed to get the game restarted, but not for long the ref was being pushed and shoved, and they said they were not going to play, if he let the goal stand, but the ref said the goal was going to stand, and that he had no alternative but to abandon the game. We had to go to the County Board again, the match was fixed to be replayed at O'Neill Park Dungannon, now this was big stuff for us, and none of us had ever played on a big pitch like this before. It was one of the places the big games would be played, such as the Ulster semi-finals or the Dr McKenna Cup. I thought it was a great privilege to be playing in a venue like this, it was late in the season, but it was a lovely day and we had great support with us. Matt O Brien and his crew had a good talk to us before the game, and just told us to believe in ourselves, and we could do it, and we did just that, we had the same referee who refereed the abandoned game, he called both teams together, and told us in no uncertain terms, that he would finish the match, if he had to finish it with two goal keepers. We won it by a point, a week later we had a big dance in the AOH hall in Aughnacloy for the presentation of the medals, and that about wrapped up the season for us, and sadly that was to be my last bit of glory for Aughnacloy football club. Something happened that was to change my whole way of life around, but before I come to those events I will go back the previous year.

The new church hall opened in Clara around August 1952, it was opened by the great Clipper Carlton Showband from Strabane, it was Irelands first Show Band, and it was just fantastic.

Father Donnelly would always be running functions in the hall, and he asked a few of us if we would do a bit of playing for him. Kevin Maguire, my brother Arthur and myself used to play quite a bit together, mostly in Maguire's house, and we would listen to Radio Luxemburg and learn the popular tunes. Anyway it was arranged that Kevin, Arthur, myself, and Wishie Finnegan would play some music for the priest. Wishie was the man with the car, which was handy as none of the rest of us had a car. Wishie played a bit on the fiddle too, but would go well with the modern tunes, I was the drummer, I borrowed the big drum from the marching band, bought a foot pedal, and got hold of an old snare drum, which I put new skins on, there were no plastic heads that time, and we went under the name of the Ivy Quintet. It was Father Donnelly who put this name on us, it should have been Quartet, but he said Quintet sounded bigger, and we could add another later. We carried on like this for a while, we were limited how far we could go, and we were depending on Wishie.

Then we heard some boys over in Ballygawley who were playing lovely music, Kevin "Larry" McKenna told us he heard them playing in an old thatched house, on the Omagh road on the left at the top Ballygawley town. We didn't have any trouble finding it, we could hear this lovely music, it sounded heavenly and we asked if we could come in, they said it was ok. There were four of them, Bob Douglas on the banjo, his brother Paddy on mandolin, he also played guitar, Tommy Robson on fiddle and Hugh Jennings on piano Accordion. There was not a lot of this kind of instrumental music being played around our part of the country, it was like a breath of fresh air.

These lads did not play in many places, which was a pity because they were really good, but they didn't bother to put themselves about to look for bookings, after a while the broke up. That's when we got in touch with them, and asked if they would play with us, so they said they would, but we only looked for halls not far away, because of lack transport. We were not too bad north of the border, because Bob and Paddy had vans which belonged to the people they worked for, but they just could not travel too far over the country, our bookings were limited a bit but it was a start.

We named our band, The Valley Band. I bought my self a new drum kit, I don't know where I got the money from for the high hat cymbals, it was a lot of stuff to haul about if you didn't have transport of your own. It was all a bit trial and error and a bit of good luck.

Amplifiers were another concern, at time a lot of the country halls did not have electricity so you needed a special kind that could be driven by a car battery. The dances started around nine pm until 3 am, so you needed two car batteries to last the night. We did not have our own amps so we used to hire from McGirrs in Ballygawley. There would be two speakers fixed half way down the hall, one on each side of the hall, it's hard to imagine what it was like in those times, we were just a few country lads having fun, we had a great little band once we got a few tunes sorted. It was different from other bands that were about, Paddy could play the steel guitar, or the Hawaiian guitar as it was called in those days, and it was something you would not see in many bands at that time. They would stop dancing and come to the stage and watch him play, he didn't have it on a stand like they do now, he had it resting across his knee he was great on the acoustic guitar, and the mandolin, he was a brilliant musician. We used to play quite a lot for the Parish Priest in the parochial hall in Aughnacloy, as I said earlier, neither Kevin, Arthur, nor I had cars. My brother Felix had a car, but he did a lot driving all over the place, like farmers going to cattle markets and such, so you would have to be lucky to catch him at home.

These dances in the parochial hall would be held on a Friday night, this time we could not see any hope of having any transport, and we knew we would have to do it the hard way. Paddy and Bob both had vans but you could not take a vehicle across the border without having what was known as a bond on it. In other words it was like a kind of bail, if you lived in Northern Ireland you would need someone in the Republic to go bond for you or vice versa, so it was up to us to get our instruments in by a bit of donkey work. I brought the drums from Dromore to the place where I worked and slept there, I had done this on the night before the dance. Arthur and I arranged to meet at Brushes Lane the following night, which was the lane that led up to the house where I worked and lived. The lane was about a half mile long, I tied the bass drum on my back and tied all the bits and pieces to the bicycle but could not ride the bicycle until I got to the end of the lane where I was to meet Arthur, who was bringing the rest of stuff with him. Then we would reorganize things around, there was a little embankment at the end of the lane, the plan was I would put one foot on the embankment, and then get the other leg over the cross bar, and sit on the bicycle while Arthur loaded me up. I had the bass drum tied on my back, then I tied both ends of a piece of cord to the snare drum, put the cord over my head and round the back of my neck. Which left the snare drum resting on my chest, Arthur was fully loaded as well, he had an accordion in one hand, and one strapped on his back and the banjo in the other hand. He would be the one to dismount first, it was about a mile from the end of the lane to Aughnacloy where we were going to play, it was not a comfortable journey, our pockets were stuffed with different bits and pieces, and however we made it to the hall. We had one bit of luck, we just managed to get our stuff inside the hall, just before it started to pour down with rain. I suppose you could say good luck in one way, and bad luck in another way, because not many people turned up, except some locals from the town, we were depending mostly on people from the country but the weather upset that.

We played away all night, we enjoyed playing and even though there was a small crowd they enjoyed the night as well. By the end of this night, when all was sorted out, all we had left was one shilling and six pence each. We didn't think much of money, Father Moan was a lovely man, and always paid our fee whatever we asked for, so we didn't mind we had the honour of playing, I would do it all again. We played in quite a few local places as we were we were inhibited because of lack of transport, and we had some great house parties around Christmas, and I enjoyed every minute of it.

CHAPTER 17

RELUCTANT RUNAWAY

GOING BACK TO the other events throughout 1953, the man I worked for gave me the use of a field for the season, so as I could grow some flax for myself, to make extra money for myself, but that was not as easy as it seems. I had to do his work, and look after my own field of flax as well. As I explained earlier, unlike corn or wheat flax had to be pulled by hand, there were some flax pulling machines but they were not much of a success, flax was not something that you could let drag on days or weeks, it needed to be pulled, drowned and worked within a few days. It was the usual custom in our part of the country to do what was called swapping, you go to as many people as possible before or after your flax pulled, then they would return the complement. You would always near enough know, how many men you would need to do the job. Flax seed was measured in pecks, then for instance if you sowed twelve pecks, twelve good men would be able to pull that in a day, unlike corn or wheat you could pull flax even if it was raining, providing the men were willing to do so. But the problem I had was that I didn't have much time to make many swaps, which meant that I had to pay some men, but this was not very successful, it started to rain about an hour after we started on the first day, the men I hired stopped and stood under a tree till it eased up, then came out and did another bit, and so on till half the was gone, then they went home, and I still had to give them a full day's pay.

After a few days I managed to get my field of flax pulled, thanks mainly to the help of my two cousins Big Peter and Patrick Sherry from Derrylevick and Francie "Nail" Mc Kenna, without this kind of help, I would have lost it all. I remember saying, "that's the last beet of flax I will ever pull," I had just about had enough.

Now that the pulling was over and done, the hard work was far from over, if you didn't get it into the dam within a few days it would spoil, it was a very big job for two men but a near impossible job for one man, because you had to get it all into the dam and get it submerged or "drowned" on the same day, as I have said before this was done by putting weight of some kind, preferably stones or sods of earth, or both, this was normally at least a four man job, one man on cart building a load and another man pitching up to him, The load would be tipped off at the dam, so you would not be able to get very close to the dam, that's where the third man came in, he had to pitch the flax over to the man who was putting the flax into the dam, I did not know how or what way I was going to get it done, if it had been my brother Peter, Mum would have the whole family mustered, all I could do was to stick with it and get on with things, I was now at my lowest ebb, and then help arrived in the person of Hugo Douglas, it just seemed heaven sent, god bless him. I am forever grateful to him, the little pony, and the flat top cart he brought with him, it was just what I needed to do the job, and at last it seemed that someone cared. The field where we had taken flax, was on a hill, and would have been a lot harder and slower if we had to use heavier horse and cart, as the ground was wet, the little cart just floated over the wet ground, he was able to load the flax on the cart himself and bring it to the dam, I put the flax in the dam, and while waiting for him to come back with another load, I cut some sods, so we would have it drowned as quickly as the field was cleared of flax, and we had all this done in daylight, it was a hell of a day's work for two men, as I mentioned above it was a four man job.

Changing Lanes

Now the next big job, in about ten days' time, would be taking the flax out of the dam again and spreading it, the spreading would be done over a meadow or a field that was clear of weeds or thistles. Then if the weather was good, it would be lifted and tied in beets, and then "stooked", and after a while, built into a stack. After all this, then you needed to see the flax mill owner, and book a date to have it scutched, but there was a lot of hard work in-between, and once again, help was very scarce. Taking the sods or stones off was a massive job, at the very least a two man job, I was once again on my own, then my cousin Paddy Sherry turned up and gave me a hand, he was only a young lad at the time, but was always willing to help someone out, but he had to go about half way through to do someone else a good turn, it was dark when I finished. I then got the horse cart out, and worked half way through the night scattering the beets of flax over the fields where it was to be spread, I was lucky there was a bit of moonlight, which helped me a lot.

I got up early next morning, it was Sunday, I went to eight o'clock mass in Aughnacloy, came home, harnessed the horse, and scattered the remainder of the flax, and then set out to spread on my own. Then after a while, my boss Tom came out and helped me, it took all the next day to get it all spread, eventually I managed to get it all lifted, tied, "stooked" and stacked. I built the stack myself, my Sister Florence pitched the beets up to me, I had not built a flax stack before, my brother Peter would nearly always do the building, I was a bit wary at the start, it was always looked upon as a specialist job, I knew how to do it, but just never got around to doing it. It was a massive big stack, as it got higher, we had to put a ladder up against the stack, Florence would have to stick the pitch fork into a beet of flax, and walk up few steps of the ladder, but between us, we got it built as good as the experts, then it had to be thatched and roped. Florence stayed with me till all this was done, I wonder if she can remember all this. It was a grand days work all round, the next move would be to try and get a place booked in the flax mill before Christmas. I tried but the mill owner told me that it would be after Christmas, as he was fully booked up, anyway I managed to get in shortly after Christmas, and got it scotched, and it done really well, it was a yield of over twelve stones to the peck, it was good flax growing land. Now at this time, the price of flax in the south was lower than the north, but people from the south were allowed to take flax over to the north and have it scutched, but were not allowed to sell it in the north, they would have to take it back and sell it in the south. This was a concession given by both Governments, as there were fewer flax mills in the south, and it would be a longer wait to get their flax scotched. It didn't take a lot of working out that this was going to be exploited. Ever since this was the setup, there were always people to take advantage to make a few pounds, but more often than not, it was to do a neighbour a good turn.

Now I had finished with the last of the flax, or maybe not quite all of it, I was back in the routine of what farm work was about. It was the day of the Aughnacloy market, and we had just slaughtered four pork pigs for the market, which was one the things I hated most about farming, but it had to be done, and a man called Jimmy McCrudden, our regular butcher a good man at his job, came to do the business. We took them to the market, and the next day, had them weighted and paid for. We came home, had a good meal, and I was well pleased with myself, but not for long. I looked out the window, and saw a man coming up the lane, I knew that he was he was an official of some kind, I thought he might be from the national insurance, all the years I worked for Tom he had never stamped any cards for me, he said he could not afford it, and I was not earning enough money to pay tax, so I had nothing much to worry about, I done nothing wrong, but I thought he might get into trouble for not stamping cards for me, so I ducked into my room hoping that Tom might say that I was not there, so I would have a bit of time to sort things out, but I should have known better, as Tom would hardly tell a lie to save his own life, so he was not going to start now. I was listening to hear what the man would say when Tom opened the door, he asked does James Sherry live here, and Tom just shouted out, "Jimmy", so I had to go out and talk him, he said he was from the ministry of agriculture, and according to their records I had grown some flax on this land, I said that was correct, that I had, then he said we have reasons to believe that the yield of your flax is far in excess for the acreage it was grown on, he asked me to show him the field it was grown on, and if flax was all grown on that field, he was trying catch me out, the minister of agriculture knew the acreage of every field that flax was grown on, because they paid the owner of the land a subsidy each acre flax grown, he then said he had reason to believe that there were two different fibres in my lot, and that some of it must have been grown elsewhere, then he warned that I could be subject to a heavy fine, or imprisonment, or both. Then he said "oh, by the way how many stone of flax did you have?, I said "I thought you knew that already", "I want you to confirm how many stone you had", I told him I couldn't remember, he looked at me and said, "you only sold this flax less than three weeks ago, do you expect me to believe that", then he said I would be hearing from them again very shortly.

The reason I got into this trouble was that, on the night I went to the mill and got paid for my flax, as I was about to go out through the door, the mill owner said, "Oh I put a few stones of another man's flax in along with yours", he did tell me the man's name, but I better not mention any names, not to know what I was getting myself into, I said "that's OK", you would always like to do a neighbour a good turn, but I should have been told beforehand, or should I say, I should have been asked, I was in right state of turmoil, if I had to go to court, there was no way I was to swear lies, so I said to myself, there is only one thing to do, and that was to clear off to England, and then nobody would be in any trouble. I went to see the Mill owner, but he did not have any easy solution, but I didn't tell him that I was going to England, I went round home that night to get my suit and a shirt and best shoes, I said I had toothache and that I was going to the dentist the next day. I stayed at home that night, but could not sleep a wink worrying about how my mother was going to take it. I went back to my place of work and told Tom that I had to go to the dentist, he said go as soon as you are ready, I said I had a few jobs to do first, I brought enough potatoes in from the field to last a week, and got enough hay ready for the two animals. I made the hay up into was called wopes, and cut enough sticks to last several days, just to try and make it a bit easy for the poor man. I really I felt so bad about the whole thing, leaving Tom like this, but I was at breaking point, I could not see any other way out.

There was nothing more I could do, so I got washed, shaved and dressed, and ready for the off, Tom was on the street outside, he asked is it giving you a bit of pain, I said it was, because truthfully, I was in terrible pain, but not from the tooth, but from my heart and soul, I am sure the look on my face must have said it all, Tom said, "ah well, you'll feel better when you get it sorted", he said, "are you off now?", I said I was, and I got on my bike and rode down the lane for a bit, then got off just where the little rowing boat used to be tied up, I stood and looked back at the house, it was my life, my home, I grew up there, I spent over twelve happy years there, I scanned all around the fields, meadows and hills, the cattle that I fed that morning, my favourite horse and dog were dead and gone, if they had been there, maybe I might not have gone.

I got on my bike and headed for Aughnacloy the tears were streaming down my face, I stopped further down the lane, went to the edge of the river and splashed some water over my eyes to calm myself down a bit, at least I was well dressed, if I been going to the dentist like I said I was, I am sure I would have been the best dressed person there. Aughnacloy was my next stop, I knew Hugo Douglas would nearly always be in Aughnacloy between twelve and one o'clock, and sure enough he was, he was going out with my sister Florence at the time, I told him what I was going to do, and I warned him not to tell anyone until late that night, when hopefully I would on the boat from Belfast by that time, I asked him to take the bike out home for me, on the way into Aughnacloy, I stopped and talked to Kitty Sherry my cousins wife, and asked her if she knew Pat Sheridan's address in Birmingham, she said she did, she wrote it out on an envelope for me, I said I had promised to drop him a few lines sometime, but had never got around to it, I told her the same story that I was going to the dentist, having Pats address was good news, it would make it a bit easier for me, providing he hadn't moved.

My bus to Belfast was leaving at one o'clock, Hugo took me into Paddy Campbell's and bought me a glass of whiskey, we had a bit of a chat, we said goodbye, and off I went. I got into Belfast around four o'clock. I thought I would take a little walk up the Whiterock road, to the place where we ran our first cross country race at Corrigan Park, it brought back good memories, on my way back, who did I meet, but my little friend Tommy O'Neill, whom I used to work with. It was nice to meet him again, especially at a time like this. He took me to his digs, and his landlady said she would put me up, if I did not get to the boat on time, she was a very kind lady, she made some tea for me. I gave her ten Shillings for a room for the night, and said I would call back later and let them know how I got on. Then I made my way to the docks to find the time of the boats. They told me that the boat was sailing at nine, so I had plenty of time, I went back to see my friend Tommy again, his landlady offered to give me my money back, which I refused to accept, she insisted on making me some sandwiches, which I was very grateful for, they helped me on my journey, I said goodbye and went on my way. It was nice to see Tommy again, it brought back memories of the good times we had when we were working for Tom Brush, and my whole way of life changed from that day on. I think back to the Summer of that year, it could have made a decision like this quite easier, I found it very hard to get much help, except from a few reliable friends, however I had made my decision, and there was no turning back now, I just wanted to get on that boat and get out of the Country. I had this silly feeling, that someone would waiting for me at the boat, and try and talk me out of going, looking back at it afterwards, that would be very unlikely, anyway I made it to the boat, but I didn't think things over well, instead of booking a ticket all the way to Birmingham, I had just booked a single ticket to Heysham, When I got off the boat everyone else was rushing to the train, while I had to go looking for the ticket office, I was in a bit of panic in case I missed the train, as it turned out, I had plenty of time, it was a long lonely journey to New street station in Birmingham, and I just could not manage to get off to sleep.

When I got there, I think it was late morning, but I didn't have a clue how to get to Pat's address, everyone seemed to be in a hurry. I thought my best plan would be to show someone the envelope with the address on it, if I could manage to get someone to stop long enough. However, eventually I managed to get there. I knocked on the door, this big English woman comes out, I asked her if there was anyone by the name of Pat Sheridan living there, she said there was, and asked me if I wanted to speak to him, she was quite a pleasant lady, she said I was in luck as he was off work because of the frosty weather. She went back inside and Pat came out to the door, when he saw me, his eyes nearly popped out, he didn't expect to see me standing on his step in Birmingham. I told him why I was there, and asked him if there was any chance that his landlady could put me up for a while, Pat said, "leave it to me, I will have a word with her", he came back rubbing his hands, he said, "I think you will be alright, she will see you herself in a few minutes", she came back out and said, "if you don't mind sharing with Pat, I can put you up, I will show the room first, and you can see for yourself, I had look, and told her it was OK, she said it would be two pounds per week in advance, I wasn't too fussy, I just needed a place to stay, it was frosty and cold outside, and I was delighted to have a place to stay. It was a lovely comfortable room, things were different in those days, sharing a room in those days was quite the done thing, no-one thought anything of two men sharing a room, anyway it was common practice in those times to share room and a bed. Pat was a neighbour from back home, we were all brought up rough and ready so it didn't bother me in the least, Pat was a great friend and a great help to me.

So far everything was going well for me. Now the next important thing for me to do was to find a job, the day was still early, so Pat took me down to the labour exchange, what people now would call, the job centre, to register for work. There was a job going in a glass bottle factory, I was working with a whole crew of women there were about ten or twelve of them, their job was to pack bottles into crates, these would then be collected by different breweries and pubs, my job was to keep the women supplied with the empty crates and then move the full crates to a suitable place for collection by trucks or trains, depending on where they had to go, it was a lovely job, I loved it, and thought I was very lucky to get it, as there were a lot people out of work from the building sites. I must say I was delighted the way things turned out for me, a great start, on my first day of arrival, and I had got myself a place to stay, landed myself a job, and this was on a Friday, they asked me to start the next morning, which was quite unusual to start on a Saturday, but I was not complaining, and my job was only about ten or fifteen minutes away from where I lived, so I could walk to work, there was also a good bus service. Pat took me to a big market place called the Bullring, you could buy just about anything there. I bought some working clothes and boots, all this on my first day there. So I said to Pat I would like to go back to the digs and sit down and write a few lines to my mother. So I did just that, and got the letter posted, at that time it could take a letter a week to go from England to Ireland, and nobody had telephones in those days, so a great day's work had been done, now we ready for a night out on the town. Pat took me around a few different clubs, we finished in a club called St Catherine's.

The place was full, and there a nice Irish band playing Irish music, the hall was upstairs, and you could see all the lights all over the city, it was lovely, and I was happy, and said to myself, this is the place to be, it was the first decision I was ever allowed to make on my own. I would have liked to have done it better, but I didn't have the time, I felt so bad not being able to let my girl know, and also Tom, I just had to do it the way I did, I said I was happy, but the sadness and guilt kept coming back to haunt me, when I thought of the good people and good things I had left behind me, I was involved in a lot of things that I liked doing, such as the Aughnacloy Gaelic Football Club, which meant so much to me, the Glaslough Harriers, the marching band, and lots of other things, sometimes I thought maybe I should have made this move years ago, but I then I would have missed so many good times, and my life would have been very different.

Well I was here now, and enjoying it, I enjoyed going to the dances, but I was expecting bands to be playing more modern music, like the bands back in Ireland were playing, bands like Clipper Carleton and Melody Aces would be playing all the modern music. I began to think it might not be too hard to get into a band over here, I could play the accordion, and I had done quite a bit of drumming, and a bit of singing, then one night the drummer in one of the bands took ill at short notice, they were asking around the hall if there was anyone who could drum, so Pat told them about me, they asked me it I would help them out, they said the other drummer be off for a few weeks, I said I would be glad to help and I fitted in well, I knew nearly all their songs and tunes, and I was very happy doing what I loved doing, and I was under my own control.

Then the first letter arrived from my mother, and then followed by letters from all the rest of the family, saying how they all missed me, and hoping it would not be long until I would be back home to stay. Everyone wanted to help now, but in the previous year that help was very scarce when I needed it most. I vowed then that there would have to be changes in the coming year, but I didn't intend it to happen the way it did, thinking back maybe it was all for the best the way it happened, I would have found it very hard to tell Tom that I would soon be leaving him.

CHAPTER 18

ON THE ROAD AGAIN

When I arrived in England and got myself nicely sorted out, I had no intention of going back to Ireland for at least a year, but this not going to work out the way I had hoped. My Sister Nellie was getting married in July, so there was no way I could not go to the wedding, so that was the first hiccup, then there were other plans being put in motion for me, other people seemed to know what was better for me than I did, the control thing was beginning to resurface again.

My sister Maggie lived in Gillingham. Kent, in the south east of England. She wrote to me to tell that there was a big job started on the Isle of Grain, they were building a big oil refinery there, and the wages were great. She had all the information, she kept lodgers at time, and most worked on this job, so she seemed to know the ins and outs, but I was very happy where I was, I knew quite a few people from back home, I didn't like the thought of moving again, but once my mother got to know about this great job, the pressure was on, I knew it would madness not to go after one these jobs, I could go down to Gillingham and stay with Maggie, where I would be well looked after, and I could earn a lot of money, and after a while, I could go back to Ireland, nobody seemed to have any idea of the reality of it all, but once again I gave in too easy. I decided to give it a try, although honestly, I was very unhappy about the whole thing.

Maggie, her husband Sid and Dermot their son, who was only a little boy at the time, met me in London and brought me down to Gillingham. So I had to start all over again, and find my way about, and try and find new friends, it was winter time, and not a good time to be looking for work, Maggie had given me the impression that all I had to do, was to go out and get started straight away, but it wasn't like that at all, Sir Robert MacAlpine had his own method of hiring and firing, sometimes he would fire five hundred men on a Thursday, and then within a few weeks, take the same amount back again. So it was four or five weeks before I got started, but then I was luckier than some there, a man staying in Maggie's, who kept a look out for me, he was a really nice chap, his name was Joe Keady, he was Scottish and he had a great sense of humour. I used to enjoy a drink with him, anyway he came home one Friday night and told me that MacAlpine was taking men on, the following Monday, so I went out there and got started, and became one of "McAlpine Fusiliers". The song that Dominic Behan wrote, and was made famous by the Dubliners, named after the men who worked for McAlpine in those days, contains a line, "I was stripped to the skin with the darkie Finn, way down upon the Isle of Grain, with "horseface" O'Toole well you knew the rule, no money if you stopped for rain", and I remember horseface O'Toole from when I worked on the Grain, and it was the right way to describe him. It certainly was an eye opener, there were thousands of men on the site, the site was three miles square, and quite easy to get yourself lost, I had never worked on a building site before, and this was certainly an eye opener. It was hard work, now I wasn't afraid of hard work, it was just getting to know the names of different tools, and getting the slang words, I often said to myself, "why didn't I stay in Birmingham where I was happy and had everything going for me?", but it was another experience, looking back now, I am glad I had it, it was one of many in my lifetime, it gave me a broader outlook on life, all the different kind of people I met, the good, the bad and the ugly, but the majority of them were good people. I think about people who have had only one job in their lifetime, I suppose they counted themselves lucky, and maybe

Changing Lanes

they were, but you don't get to meet as many people and different characters, I think you get a better look at what life is about, I think it makes you more able to cope with whatever challenges you might meet throughout your life.

It didn't take me too long to get the hang of things, the work was hard but the money was good, we had a lot of extras on top of our basic rate, such as height money and dirt money, but only in certain conditions. We also had free transport, we got a free travel voucher every eight weeks, I used to give some of them to my sister and she could use them to travel to Ireland. Getting back to the free transport, the buses and couches were supplied by different transport companies, they were not always in top class condition, we didn't mind if they broke down in the morning, we would get paid for it, but getting home in the evening, the buses would be racing each other to get out in front, the lads would all be shouting and urging the drivers on, there were only certain places at which they could pass one another, sometimes someone would finish up in the ditch, it was like the wild west in the gold rush days.

I decided to stay in the camp when I first started, to save having to travel every day, but this really was like the wild-west, there would be drinking and gambling and fights nearly every night, until the money ran out. You could get "the sub" on Tuesday and Friday if you needed to, "the sub" was an advance on your wages, and we got paid on Thursday. I didn't like the idea of subbing, I didn't really want to, but then if some of the boys saw that you were not subbing, they would assume you had a lot of money and would be, "tapping you up", for money, so sometimes it was wise to have the odd small sub, to keep them from pestering you. It was sad to see men wasting their hard earned money on gambling and drink, and I'm sure some of them had parents back home in Ireland who could be doing with a few pounds. I remember one young lad, he was always talking about saving up enough money to go home and see his parents, he had his case all packed and ready to go next morning, he sat down to have a game of poker, but didn't stop until all the money was gone, he even sold his travel voucher, I don't know if he ever made it home, about this time I decided I had had enough of the camp, and went to stay with Maggie in Gillingham.

Working conditions were not very good, the toilets were little wooden huts, three foot wide and four foot long, and about seven foot six tall, with a wooden bench seat with a hole in it, and the famous helsen bucket in the hole. These buckets would be emptied every day, there was a special gang who did this, they got extra money and protective clothing, and a special washing room, you can imagine what these toilets would look like, and smell like, on a summers day, or any day for that matter, there was a lot to be said for the open field back home in Ireland. The washing facilities were not good either, there was a metal trough fixed onto metal posts, it was about thirty yards long, there was a pipe fixed to the trough with turn on taps fixed every few feet, it was all cold water, and no special hand wash, just a few barrels of sand, you could grab a handful and rub it on your hands to get some of the grime off your hands, there were also some concrete troughs, with the head of a broom bolted to them, where you could rub your boots, or "wellies", there was also a water tap fixed there. We were only allowed three minutes washing time, you could go home without washing, but your land lady might not take too kindly to you. I was alright, I had an old shed which I could change in, The first evening I came home I was covered in rust, we were cleaning tanks that were full of rust, I was like a red Indian, a bath was the only cure for this. Sir Robert MacAlpine did not have any time for unions, so there was not much we could do to change things, We did manage to get together once, this was about getting an afternoon tea-break, we managed to get together and marched to the town hall in Chatham as a protest, after that we got a ten minutes tea-break in the afternoon, but you were not allowed to sit down. I suppose it was better than nothing, but they were not an easy bunch to organise, most of them didn't want to know.

By now I had settled in well, and had got to know a lot of the lads, we would meet at the weekends and go to dances, we had great fun while it lasted, Then I had a letter from my mother telling me that Nellie was getting married in a few months' time, and that I would have to come over for it, I did not have a problem about going to the wedding, but I knew what the story would be, when everything would be over, and I would going back to England again, everyone would be trying to find a job for me. I stayed at home in Ireland for nearly three months after the wedding, and spent most of the money I had earned. My Brother Arthur, who built the new house at home in Dromore, was finishing off the house at that time, so I gave him a bit of a hand putting up the scaffolding, it was not like the scaffolding we use nowadays, it was wooden poles and wooden brackets, they were L shaped with three pieces of timber fixed unto the vertical one, and three pieces of timber fixed to the horizontal timber, which formed like a little trough in which the long wooden poles fitted into, and this would be used to move brackets up down the wall to whatever height you required the platform to be. You required at least two of these brackets so as you could lay the planks across from one to the other, and of course a ladder was needed to get onto the platform it would not meet the safety requirements of the present day, and I don't think there were any more accidents then than there are now, people then had a lot of good common sense.

My brother Arthur was only eighteen years of age at this time, it was just amazing the work he did on that house, he drew the plans out himself, and it was just unreal. He had to carry all the materials up a ladder, a neighbour man Jim O'Hagan helped him to put the roof on, and another man, his name was Jimmy Sherry, he was known by the name of Jimmy Fat, that was what his nick name was, he was not related to our family, he was a great carpenter, he helped Arthur with the windows and stairs.

There was nothing easy about any of this kind of work, he was now about to do something he had never done before, or had anyone else for that matter, up until now a lot houses would be pebble dashed, or plastered in a smooth surface all over, or some might be marked out in the shape of blocks. Then a new product came on the market, it was called Terralene, it was a powder similar to cement, it would be mixed in water in small amounts, as the machine which was used to spray it onto the wall was not very big, but simple enough to operate. There was rotating handle on the side of container with a carrying handle on top, and it was open at the front. Inside the device the rotating handle on the side, was attached to a little drum inside, which had a number of little metal plates fixed to the drum, when handle was turned, the drum revolved, and would throw the terralene out through hole at the front, and on to the wall. All simple enough you might think, but there was quite a bit of skill in operating the little machine, it needed to be operated at the same speed all the time in order to have the same pattern on the wall, from start to finish, which also meant you needed the exact mix all the way through. Arthur was a very clever lad, and in no time at all, he got it right, in fact he made it look so simple. After a little while, he let me have a little go at it, and after a little while, even I got the hang of it. While Arthur carried on with work I would be doing some painting, from time to time, the scaffolding would have to be moved, either upwards, downwards or sideways, and this was the hardest part of the job. Anyway like most jobs it seems easier after a while, but my time was running out, my friend Pat Sheridan was home from England, so I got talking to him, and told him that I was thinking about going back to Birmingham, and asked him if there much work available. He said it was fairly good, so I decided there and then, that was where I wanted to be. Then another old pal of mine, Joe Woods, called to see me and, said that he was thinking about going to England, I told him the date Pat and myself had arranged, so he said he would try and arrange the date, and come along us. He was working in Belfast at this time, and he got everything sorted, and we arranged to meet him in Belfast. Everything worked out as planned, we boarded the infamous Princess Maud for Birmingham. We got there early the next day, once again, Pat was the Good Samaritan, and he asked his landlady if she could put us up for a few nights until we could find some place to stay. This was the same place that I stayed in the first time I came over. She said she didn't have any spare rooms, but said she would try and fit us in somewhere amongst the other lads. Pat was OK. he had his own room, anyway we got fixed up in an attic room, there were ten people in the room already, but she managed two more small beds for Joe and me, fair enough she was trying to help us out, she said you don't have to take this if you don't want to, but we decided we take it, we had to take into account that we had to find jobs, and we didn't yet know what part of the City we might find these jobs. We did manage to find jobs, they would nearly always give you a few days to think about it, so we would keep them on hold to see if we could find a better one, and we thought it would be nice if the three of us could be on the same job together. What we all wanted was an inside job, as winter would soon be upon us, we were lucky we finally got one that suited us, and they agreed to start all three of us, the money was better than any of the other jobs. Most people would have been over the moon to get a job like this, but none of us had any intention of settling there for a long term, we decided to take the job, the place was called, Morris Commercial Cars Ltd, it was what they call a doddle, a bit boring at times, there never seemed to be enough work to keep you going, and sometimes they might ask you work over-time in the evenings. Joe and myself were in the same side of the factory, but would rarely see each other during day, and Pat was further away in different part of the works, we all started and finished at same time and got the same bus to and from work to get back to our accommodation. We only stayed few days in the attic, it was cramped beyond belief, getting into bed was a difficult operation, you had to put everything into your suitcase, except what you were wearing in bed, push the case under the bed, and that way your things were sort of safe, and the best place for a spare of shoes, was to put one under each leg of the bed, there were some dodgy looking characters amongst them, I suppose I could say I had a little more luck than some, I could open the skylight window and stand up straight while getting dressed. Anyway we found other digs at the weekend, they were comfortable enough, Joe and me had a big room to ourselves, the bathroom was shared by the whole household, the food was a bit limited, I think maybe Pat faired a little better than us, he was only a short distance away from us. They were nice enough for a while, then I think what started it off was, there was a missionary in the Catholic Church only a few streets away, and he would be outside church when the service was over, and would be talking to everyone, and asking them if they had place to stay, and if the place you were staying was OK, just being friendly and wanting to know if you had any problems. He talked to me one Sunday and asked me where I lived, he asked me if it would alright to call and see me, he asked me my name, and the number of the house, I suppose I should have thought about it, before I said it would be alright. I told him that there was another fellow staying there as well, he said, "that's alright, I have got your name that will do", anyway two of them called in the afternoon before we got home, and I gather she didn't give them a hearty welcome. I suppose looking at it now, I was a bit out of order, I was now living in England, but still thinking the Irish way, I did apologise, I told her that I expected that we would be home before they would call, that way, we could have spoken to them at the outside, but from that day onwards she was in an unpleasant mood, she didn't have much time for us, or for catholic clergy, apparently she had some disagreement with some nuns at a school where one of her young girls were taught, anyway I didn't agree with some of the things that she said, and that did not go down too well either. Joe and I said we would stick it out until Christmas, as we would be going to Ireland for Christmas. Sometime before this, my brother Felix had wrote to me asking if it would be alright for him to come and stay with us some weekend, I asked the landlady if he could come and stay us, and she said it would alright, he arrived one weekend and she was alright about it. Felix, Joe and myself went out that night, it was a Friday night, we had a great night, everything was as usual when we got home, we went out the next night again, and when we came home everything was quiet, they seemed to be all in bed, then suddenly all hell broke loose, the place was in complete uproar things were being thrown about, this time it was glasses flying, and yorkies crying, as things were thrown around, every so often, someone would come flying against our bedroom door, it sounded like a wild west saloon brawl, it was impossible to tell who was against who, but we knew that we were part of the problem. The man of the house, little John as we used to call him, along with a few other names being a little less polite, he was miserable little toe rag, he had a little stammer, god bless him, he never used the F word, he used the word stinking to describe anything or anybody, he kept shouting about, "sti, sti, sti..ink, stinking lodgers", over and over again, so we knew we had something to do with it. It goes without saying, we did not get any breakfast the next morning, as we were going out the next morning, there was a pile of broken glasses, and whatever swept up in the middle of the floor, we all decided to eat out somewhere on that day, we didn't go back into the house until late that night We were wondering what the atmosphere would be like when we would arrive home from work Monday afternoon, but things were no worse or no better so we could live with that. Then things took another turn, they bought themselves an old car, but none of them had a driving licence, so they needed someone to take them about, and maybe give some driving lessons, they knew Joe had a driving licence, so they asked Joe if he would take them out for a few runs, in other words teach them to drive. Joe agreed to give it go, at least he was in their good books again. Joe got a great kick out of it all, but he didn't think any of them would ever make a driver, we did not have to see end product, as we were on our way to Ireland for Christmas, and would not be going back there again.

Once again we were on board the Princess Maud, a night never to be forgotten, the wind was blowing like a hurricane, and the rain was tipping down, sometimes it would turn to sleet, it was bitter cold, there was a hold which was really meant for cattle, there was a tarpaulin covering it and the passengers were in underneath, and every so often, with rain being so heavy, it formed like wells of water on top of the tarpaulin, the wind would get underneath it, and send a flood of water gushing down on top of where the passengers were. There was no place for passengers to go to get away from this, there were people lying on the floor, you could scarcely move about without standing on someone. There were people being sick, there was sick everywhere, every time the ship rolled a wall of sick would run across the deck, over the top of the people lying down. There must have been over two hundred too many people on board, you have heard of "coffin ships", well this was as near to one as you could get. The water was splashing about through the toilets, they had barriers on the bottom of the doors in those times to keep water from flowing out onto the decks, the men were better off than the women, at least they could have a pee over the hand rail. I don't know how the women managed, it was nearly impossible to move about, the only place that was not crowded was the top deck, and that is where I spent a big part of the night, it was cold, but I preferred it to the smell of smoke and sick down below, but you needed to be careful, or you could be blown, or washed overboard. I got my back to a pole and got my arms locked around it, every time the stern dipped the water came over deck, and were left suspended in mid-air for a few seconds, when this happened the front of the boat would be out of the water, then there would be a great big shudder, I asked one of the sailors what this terrible noise was, he told it was the propeller raising above the water. After hours and hours I could see lights, and what looked like land, I thought this must be Belfast because we should have been there hours ago, then after a while the light disappeared, then someone said that it was the Isle of Man we had just passed, and till this day I don't know where it was, then after a long time we could see lights, and what looked like land, this happened a few times more, but finally the lights and land got bigger and closer, and we knew we were close to Belfast. Finally a little bit of daylight began to appear, our ordeal was nearly over, but still a lot of struggling to do, everyone down below were trying to get their suitcases ready, and get as close to the gangway as possible. It was a scary journey, more so because her sister ship, The Princes Victoria, sank just off the Antrim coast less than a year before this, with the loss of 133 lives, they said afterwards she was un-seaworthy, anyway we managed to get the rest of the journey home safely.

CHAPTER 19

ANOTHER VENTURE

My original plan was to go back to England after the two weeks were up, I always wanted to learn to drive, but I had never got the chance, while I was working at Tom Brushes I would never have a day off except Sunday, and where cars were concerned I never got a look in. I always had it in mind when I went to England that I would take up driving lessons, but had not yet gotten around to it. I used to go out with Hugo Douglas on his bread rounds. He worked for a Bakery called Eaton's, they were based in Derry, but his round covered quite a big area covering towns and a lot of countryside in south-west Tyrone. He used to say to me, it's a wonder that I never learned to drive, well I never got the chance, he said we will be finished a bit early that day, then he would let me have go at it, When we got to Ballygally he pulled into a big vacant yard, I don't know what it had been used for before, but it was a great place to make a start, there were some old empty oil drums lying around, we could be used as obstacles, I could tell by the look on his face that he was going to enjoy this. I got into the driving seat and he showed me what to do and how to do it, he knew everything there was to know about driving, he had been doing it from a very early age. After a few false starts I began to get the hang of it. The van Hugo drove was a 10cwt (1/2 ton) Morris van, it was easy enough to drive, it was

James Sherry

a spare van they gave him while his regular van was been repaired, and by the sounds this van was making it would soon need repairing, anyway he decided to let me do some driving on some quite country roads. So eventually I got behind the l wheel, I was beginning to get a bit worried as the roads were very narrow, but it was alright as long as you didn't meet anything, then you would have to pull in to let whatever it might be pass, there was bit of a drop on both sides, well I didn't meet anything, but something more scary happened, there was a big thud and sparks started flying, suddenly the rear wheel on the driver's side went running past us, Hugo got out of the van and lay down on the side of the road splitting his sides with laughter, all the nuts on the wheel had sheared off. I felt as if I was the only nut left, we managed to push the van to one side, and then went off to find a telephone, which were not very plentiful in those days. Eventually he got it sorted, and they brought his regular van out to us again, it had been repaired. Repairs didn't last very long on these rough mountain, roads none of these roads were tarred and had lots of potholes, which took their toll on all kinds of vehicles. His regular van was a much bigger vehicle it was about as wide as a bus, the engine was inside the cab, under a cover, so you had great view of the road, it was so different in those days you only had a mirror on the driving side there was no internal mirror, I began to think, will I ever be able to drive this one. Hugo was a bit of a devilish lad he was quite a fast driver, and even turning the van around it was all done in fast movements, turning around in a farm yard was his special treat, he would drive up fast to a building, and when you thought he was going to hit it, he would stop, you would be looking straight into the wall, I used to think will he get it wrong some time, but he never did thank God, but he had confidence in himself. He said to me it's about time you had a go in this one, he explained that the gearbox was different in this van, it was what people called a crash box, you had to double de-clutch, anyway I got into the driving seat, and put it into first gear, when I went to let the clutch out the van jumped into ditch When we had stopped, he had set me up nicely along the grass verge, there was a great lock on these vans, and as we had changed over he must have pulled the steering wheel around as far as it would go, as soon as I moved the van it would head for the ditch, I had to go to someone's house to borrow a spade to dig ourselves out. After that first day I did a bit of driving most days, and was getting on alright, but it was early days yet.

Then one day a van driver from another bakery waved us down and said he was short on some kind of bread, and he asked if we could help him out, that was the way that bread men helped each other, one might have too many loaves and not enough cake, they exchanged and swapped things as needed, they got talking about how their rounds were doing, and this fellow that had stopped us, his name was Alan Grant, said that he was only doing the round until they got another driver, he said he normally worked for the company as a checker, he would go out on different vans to check that they were not selling products that did not belong to the company, then he told us that they were looking for a driver for the van he was driving. Hugo said he had a man beside him here, looking for a job, by this time we calling each other by our first name, Alan then asked me where I was working, but before I got saying anything Hugo butted in and said, "he's working in England, in fact he's working where they make these vans, but he would rather stay in this Country if he could get a job", it seemed that I was not going to have much to say in the matter. Alan then said to leave it with him and he would find out if the company had anyone lined up for the job, or anyone in mind for it, for all he knew, they could have someone for it "Anyway I go back into the bakery everyday about this time, and I will look out for you", he said, and off he went. I looked at Hugo and said, "you've got to be joking, I can't even drive properly yet", and his answer was, "you will by the time the job comes up". I knew once my mother got to know about it there would be no backing away from it without a big argument, and I didn't want that, I just hoped they would get someone for the job, and that would get me out of a bad mess. I had only a few days left before I would be going back to England when Alan told us that there was someone in for the job, but he didn't know if the man would get it or not, and that it might take a while before they would know, it meant if I didn't get back in time for my job in England I would lose it, but no-one seemed to care what I thought, so I was talked into waiting a few more days. Then I heard one of the other applicants had got the job, so I said to myself, that's that, I will to go to England and look for another job, of course everyone kept saying stay another while longer. A few weeks soon went by and the next thing I knew was I had letter from Irwin's Bakery, telling me that the job that I had applied for a short time ago, was now vacant again and that they were willing to arrange an interview for me if I was still interested, so I reluctantly said I would give it a try. I wrote them and asked them to arrange an interview for me, and they arranged one for me in about two weeks' time, I had come so far I might as well go all the way and give it a good try.

The day of the interview came round and off I went I was quite relaxed, to me it didn't matter which way it went. Mr Irwin was very friendly and I felt very much at ease, he talked about a lot of different things, for example, where I worked in England, and what I did there. I told him the last place I worked in was the factory where they made Morris cars and vans, he said, "I suppose you know all about vans then", I said the only thing I know is how to drive one. He said his name was Kenneth, but that I could call him Kenny, and should he call me James or Jimmy. He said he felt I was the right man for the job, and the job was mine if I wanted it. I signed on conditions of employment, I was to start the next Monday morning, and there was a fifty pounds deposit for the van, this was a lot of money in those days, we shook hands and he said, "Well we'll see you Monday morning". I was beginning to dread the coming Monday morning, Hugo left me down to the depot, one good thing about it though, was that Alan Grant was the man who would be out with me to show me around, he would be out with me for two weeks, or thereabouts. He told me all about the different people, he told me about one family in particular, he said they give you breakfast every Tuesday and Friday, and not to ever refuse it, or they would be offended, and to always try and get there about the same time each day, when you arrive they will come out and invite you in for breakfast, the full Irish on

Tuesday, and boiled or scrambled eggs on Friday, because they knew I was a catholic, and they had the same themselves, they were great people, great customers. Beatty was their name, Mr Beatty was the grand Master of the Bawn Orange Lodge. I used to sell some grocery and different things, I made more profit from that, than from the bread, and it was a big help to the customers as well. I would buy them wholesale in Dungannon, and make a nice profit. One day Mr Beatty said to me, "can I take a few minutes of your time", he said that from the last week in June, until after the twelfth of July, that they had regular functions in the Orange Hall and that needed a lot of food, "I was wondering, would you be willing to help us out?, I would let you know in good time, and would make out an order for what we needed", he then said, "there are one or two of our people against giving the order to you, but I told them, there was no reason why we should not give the order to you, as you were a very obliging fellow and that you do me lots of favours, like picking things in town, and bringing them out to me, so I told them that was the end of the story" and so he gave me the order. He loved marching bands, I told him that I played in a marching band, and that we were holding a big parade in Dungannon on the fifteenth of August, "Oh, I would love to see your band", he said, "if I can get a lift I will go in and see you", he asked, "whereabouts in the band do you play, front, back or middle", I told him I was in the front row, he said, "right, if I get in I'll be looking for you", and sure enough, he made it, the streets in Dungannon are very narrow and I heard someone calling my name, and it was him, some people might find that story hard to believe!!

Alan filled me in well on what different people were like, he would get out first and talk to them they would usually ask what religion I was, so they would know who they were dealing with. One day we were going in towards a farmhouse, Alan said these are good customers, in other words, he was telling me to look after them, I could see two men filling a trailer with farmyard manure, anyway one of them looked around, and I recognized him, I said to Alan, "I can't go near him, we had a row the last we met, we had to be separated on the football field, he went a bit heavy on one of our young lads, and

I had some words with him, it was near to coming to blows, but they pulled us apart before any blows were struck", Alan said he would have a word with him, "I'm sure he will be all right", I said to Alan, "don't you see what he's got in his hand", he had this big grape that he was filling the manure with, and on his home ground. Alan told him what I had said, and he asked Alan what was my name, when Alan told him my name, he said he, "remembered the so and so, don't worry, I won't give him any trouble, tell him to come out and see me". I got out of the van, and he came walking quickly towards me with the grape in his hand, then he stopped, stuck grape into manure heap, and came over and shook my hand, and said with a grin on his face, "I remember you alright, you were a hardy wicked little hoor", and then, "let's forget all about it, I'm pleased to have you as our bread man", and from that day onwards we got on fine, I would have a mug of tea and a sandwich most days when I called there, I would never be hungry or thirsty in this part of the country. I was well treated on both sides of the divide, some people would say how did you manage to get the job or did someone pull some strings for you. If it was South of the border, then maybe that would be more likely, because I know it did happen there, all I had was three good references and fifty pounds deposit, one of the references from a protestant, a man that I had worked for 12 years, and the other two were from Catholics. I only had only one little unpleasant moment, it was on the morning before the twelfth of July, and we would all be having the next day off, as the twelfth was bank holiday in the north, and all the shops would be closed, which meant we would have extra deliveries to make, everyone was rushing about, trying get loaded as early as they could, I went into the office to pay my money in. When I was finished, and came out through the door, one of the men was waiting for me, he said, "come and have a look at your van", the fellows name was Joe Carr, he also had a brother called Barney who worked there, they were both Catholics. The weather had been good for a good while, and there was a lot dust on all the vans, but all over my van was written, "No Pope here!" There was only one entrance in or out from the bakery yard, Joe said to me to drive the van into to entrance and put keys in my pocket, so no-one could get in or out, and I did just that and went back and told Mr Irwin what had happened, and that the van was parked in the entrance, and it would stay there until everything was sorted out. He told me to take a seat, and told one of the girls to make me a cup of tea while he sorted this out. I could tell he was fuming, it was not very long before he came back in again, he apologized to me and said, "I don't know who did this, but when I find out, they will be severely dealt with, and this is what I have in mind, we will put your van on the wash, have it washed and polished, so as there will be no trace of the writing left, your van will loaded for you, and will be the first out of the yard, that is the best I can do for you", so we agreed on that, in fact, at the end of the day whoever did this, did me a good turn, I was out and away long before anyone else had left the yard. I am almost sure that it was not any of the drivers, there was someone from another department whose attitude seemed to have changed from being friendly, to not so friendly after the incident, I had some kind of a feeling, but there was never anymore said about it.

Getting back to learning the round, everything was going fairly well, Alan had the names of people written down in a little book, and names of roads and cross roads and lanes with a red gate and with a green gate and so on, he stayed with me for nearly two weeks, which was a good thing for me, I got to know all my customers, but I was still kind of dreading when I would have to go out on my own. Eventually that day arrived I managed to cope fairly well, but it took me a lot longer to get the complete hang of it, groping about and looking in the little book, but I got better as the weeks went by. Everyone was very nice towards me. After I got to know the area better, and the people to know me, some began to ask me to do them little favours, such as taking their wireless battery into Dungannon to get it charged for them, most of the country houses at that time didn't have electricity, so their wireless operated a wet and dry battery. As time went on, I would have quite a few batteries, and there were lots of other little favours, I was only too pleased help them. I began the process of building up my round, there would sometimes be sons and daughters getting married and moving to a new home within my area, I would end up adding them to my customer list. In a short time I managed to make it into a good business, you had to avail of every opportunity, for instance someone might want a birthday cake or for a special occasion in a hurry, or a certain day, or at a certain time, sometimes you would have to put yourself out to do this, but it would always pay dividends. In the end, other people would get to know about this, and would make a similar request, this was the sort of thing that built up your round, and also boosted up your commission, but then there would always be the other old problem, there would always be the few who could not pay you on the day, or maybe the next day either, there were only a few, and I had to pay for my bread every Monday morning, my weeks wages was not very big at the best of times. I found it quite hard after earning big money in England, if I had this job before I went to England, I suppose I would have been quite content, I liked job, I liked the people, I loved the countryside, this might seem odd coming from someone who was born and reared in the country, but maybe I did not take the time to see it in the same way, it was a lovely hot summer and I was getting sunburned through the glass window of the van.

There was one particular house I went to it was at the bottom a big hill, or a small mountain, I think they used to call it the Milix Mountains, there was a long laneway into it. The peoples name was Corbett, man and wife and two lovely children, about ten or eleven years of age, and a brother of the children's father also lived there. I thought they were very special, it was like a little piece of paradise, everything was so peaceful, the chickens would be lying with their wings spread out in the sun, and cattle lying peaceful in the shade of the trees. I always had my dinnertime before I called, Alan had told me about them, he told me, don't deal with them until you have your dinner, they loved a good chat.

Everything was going well for me, I was not putting myself out too much looking for new customers, there were other bread men in the area, and there was no way that I would dream of pinching another man's customers. One day a couple of young girls waved me to stop, I asked them if they were alright, they said they were, they had stopped me to ask if I would call at the mill, they said there were a lot of people working there, and they would like me to call so that they could buy some cakes or something nice for their lunch. I asked them if there were any other bread men calling there, and they said there wasn't. I said if that's the case I would be very pleased to call. I asked them what was the best time to call, and they said around one o'clock. I said I would do my best to get there around that time if possible, but it would only be on two days a week, and that was Tuesday and Friday, they said that was OK, and all this helped to boost my takings quite a lot, but every so often I would stop and think to myself, how long can I go on like this, I should be thinking of trying to build a home for myself, find a nice girl and get married. Lots of my pals had bits of land, or the prospect of getting something in the future, I had neither, as I said before, I was happy and I liked the job, I had the use of the van to get me about over the weekend, within reason, it was as good as having my own car. After sometime something happened that helped me to make up my mind. My brother-in-law Sid Bassett and my sister Maggie were home in Ireland along with their two children Dermot and Kathleen, I asked Sid if he would like to come out with me on the round someday, He said he would love to, he enjoyed the trip out through the countryside, we had tea in a couple of houses, he used to rib me about the girls, he would say, "I think they have got there eye on you", anyway when the round was finished, we were coming home along the Dungannon Road, a big black car came up behind us flashing his lights, then pulled out and passed us and stopped and waved us to stop, there were two men in the car, then I knew I had seen this car and these two men before, more than once, the first time was one day when I went to mass in Dungannon church. I had parked almost in front of the church, as I came out I could see that there was plenty of room, I only needed to reverse couple of feet to get out, which I did nice and steady, I knew that I lots of room behind me, then I felt as if I touched something, I got out and found this big black car right against me, a man came over and he said, "they drove right towards you when you were already reversing back", and said, "I will give you my name and address in case you need it", the driver of the black car got out and said he was very sorry it was his fault, and there was no damage done to either vehicle, so I was happy enough to stop and talk to them, I just wanted to get on with my work. I got out to talk to them, they asked me my name and address, they said they had reason to believe that I had not lived at that address for some time, I said that I been living and working in England for a time, then they asked if I had a work permit, I said that I didn't need one, and that I had lived and worked here since I left school, then he explained, that because I moved out of the Country for a period of time, you lose the right to work in Northern Ireland, and the same rule would apply to citizens of Great Britain, he then told me that I would have to apply for a work permit and this would take some time, and that would depend on the circumstances whether I would get a permit or not, I made my mind there and then that I would leave the job, I said to them, that it didn't matter I was leaving the job in a few weeks' time, they said OK, we will leave it like that. This was a sort of spur of the moment decision, I was upset and angry because I believed someone wanted me out of the job, then I thought would it be worth fighting for, when maybe some time in the near future, I would be making that same decision, it was too late in the day to inform my boss Mr Irwin, and worst of all, I had to go home and tell my Mother, and I was not looking forward to that, as usual everybody knew better than me, what I should have done, or what I should do. I said what is done is done, and that's the end of it. I called Mr Irwin early the next morning, and he asked me if I would come in that afternoon and see him, and I did just that. He said he would do everything in his power to see that I could keep my job, but I thanked him and said no, I thought it was too dangerous a road to go down, he said he was sorry to lose me, he was very pleased at how much I had built up the round in such a short time.

Now I had to go and tell customers who had been so good and kind to me, but I had to be careful not to that say that I was suspicious of anybody, I just told them that I needed a work permit and that I may or may not get one, so I didn't have much choice, but I think that even they had their suspicions that someone put the law on to me. I had my own suspicions about someone, after one of my customers told me to watch him, and that he had reasons to believe that this person did not like me, then I began to think that I had trod on his toes without knowing it. One day a customer asked me if I would do her a big favour, but I honestly did not know that she was the other persons customer as well, in fact she was really the other persons customer, but she always bought something from me every week, and was on my list when I took over the round, she also told the girls at the mill to ask me to go there. The favour she wanted, was for me to try and get a birthday cake baked for her within two days, in her own words, the day after tomorrow. I said it would be very tight for time, but I would do my utmost. I asked to write on a piece of paper what she wanted it made from, and what design and writing she wanted on it. I said I would give her order to the man who would bring my bread to me the next morning, which was Friday. On Friday the bakery made two deliveries, the evening delivery was for Saturday, I was to deliver to her house on Friday as usual. I told her that if they have it ready for Friday evening delivery that I would bring it to her then, she did not feel very hopeful, but sure enough they had it all ready, and I brought it round to her. It seems she had asked the other man to do this as well, but he said he would not have enough time, and as far as I know she told him not to call anymore, after which she bought all her stuff from me. This may or may not have been the cause of this persons dislike for me anyway it's all history now. I had a lot of unhappy customers wondering why I could not get anyone to help me, anyway I said goodbye to everyone and thanked them for being my customers, and for their kindness towards me, and I said that I was sorry to be leaving them. I really did miss them, I got so much involved in their way of life, just doing little favours for them from time to time, I was a country man myself, I understood their ways, so that was another part of my journey through life at an end.

Within a few weeks I was back in Kent again looking for another job, it was all a bit unsettling and not very profitable, I was on the lookout more or less for any kind of job just to carry me through, until I could find a better one. A lot of lads I used to know had moved away, there had been a big lay off on the Isle of Grain as the first phase was coming to an end, and nobody knew when the second phase would start. I managed to get a job with an Engineering Company called C.A.V., I didn't like it very much, there was another job going, it was only about five minutes' walk from where I was staying, so I packed the C.A.V. job in, and started in the other straight away, it was a spare driver job, similar to what I had been doing in Ireland. I was employed by the Gillingham Co-operative society, or Co-Op, sometimes I would be doing a bread round, and then I might be on the milk round. The Co-op also did catering for different functions, sometimes I would be driving the catering van, and it was a good variety. Then I asked for two weeks off at Christmas to go to Ireland again, I should have known better.

It was not long after I arrived back home until there were rumours about a job going in Monaghan County Council for a lorry driver, anyway, I didn't think that I would stand much chance of getting it, because I knew what it was like in Ireland, there would always be someone pulling the strings, and you needed to belong to the right political party, whoever was in power at the time. I didn't belong to any political party in the Republic, I had not lived there since I became of the age for voting, I always did my voting in the North.

So a few days later I mentioned that I was thinking of heading back to England, as soon as I mentioned it my mother said, "Oh why would you be wanting to do that, what about the job on the council", I could feel the strings beginning to tighten around me again. To try and give myself some breathing space I said that I was going over to Dungannon to see some friends that lived there. I spent the day visiting a few people, and at the last house I was in, when I said that I had best be going, the householder said, "oh don't be worrying yourself, the young lad will be home soon, he'll run you up home when he gets in", I said not to worry I have a few more people to see before I head away back. What I didn't know was that the "arresting officer", my brother John had been searching for me, on a mission.

Changing Lanes

He was looking for me to tell me that I needed to be in Monaghan straight away. When I got back up to Dromore my mother was in a panic, she told me that John had been down looking for me, and that I had got the job on the council, but I needed to be in Monaghan right away, and it is terrible that I couldn't be here, well I thought, everybody seems to know more about this job than I do. She said you better go and get ready, John will be down for you any minute now, unless the job has gone to someone else, I said I have nothing to get ready in, I only my best clothes home with me I didn't know where to turn. Then John arrived to the house, have you anything to take with you, but as I said, I had only my best suit and shoes home with me, I intended to be going back to England the day after tomorrow, I was not expecting anything like this. I said I don't know anything about this job, how am I going travel up and down to Monaghan every day? I don't have a bicycle anymore, I had one before I left, but where was that now? He said you don't have to worry about that at the moment, I have arranged for you to stay in Mary Treanor's, I must say it was organized to perfection. I was in a complete daze, I said, I better go and get a pair of pyjamas and a couple of towels and shaving stuff. John just stood there looking at me with a bit of a smile, he said you will be better dressed than our boss Joe Egan, so off we went to Monaghan. Going up the road, I felt like saying "stop, I don't want this job, just let me out, then I thought, I can't let John down, after all he had done, I will just have to give it a try. I had never driven a lorry before, I had driven big vans before, some of which were just as big as the lorry I was about to drive. Anyway I arrived at the Council yard, I was met by the yard foreman Ned Callan, who welcomed me to my new Job. He said he wanted me to take that lorry over there, all the plant in the yard had numbers on them, which included the lorries, the lorry that I was going to drive was number thirteen, he said, "your brother John is going to go out with you, he will show you where to go", he looked me up and down with a smile on his face and said, "could you not have found anything worse than that to wear", I glanced down realising how ridiculous my clothing was to be driving a lorry, I had a tweed sports jacket, a pair of gabardine trousers and pair of crepe soled shoes on, "no unfortunately this is the worst I have got", he just rolled his eyes at me and said nothing.

    Myself and John got into the lorry and headed out of the yard, we drove out the road to Cabra quarry near Threemilehouse, when we got there, and Ned Callan was there before us. He told me what he wanted me to do, was to reverse the lorry under the bins of the breaker and get filled up with a load of pitchen, I had no idea what pitchen looked like, and I knew better than to ask either. As I said before, I had my best clothes and shoes on me, I had been out on the muddy ground at the quarry talking to Ned Callan, when he was telling me what to, but when you walk in mud with crepe soles shoes, you just collect all the mud, and that can be a bit of a disaster. I got in the lorry, there was not much room to spare on either side as I reversed in towards the breaker. I was taking it nice and steady without touching the accelerator, I put my foot on the brake to stop to see if I was all right, suddenly my foot slipped off the brake and onto the accelerator, and the lorry shot back in a jump, there wasn't a bit of rubber on any of the peddles, and the side of my shoe was jammed underneath the brake pedal and on the accelerator. I managed to pull on the hand brake and got stopped, luckily Ned had his back towards me at the time and didn't see anything, After that I got a screw driver and cleared the mud of my shoes, and managed to draw a few more load that evening without any mishaps. I clocked off and made my way to Mary Treanors, at least I had a good place to stay, Mary was a very kind lady. It was her Sister Alice that brought me up when I was in Knockabeany, so I knew Mary from my very early years, she used to come to see Alice quite often, she used to cycle out from Monaghan.

    I went in to my room that first time at Mary's hoping to get a good night's sleep, it was a big room, but there was no window in it, the room was fine the bed and everything was comfortable, but I just felt trapped. I thought how did I ever let myself get into all this, I said to myself, all I can do is try and live with it for a while, at least I knew where I would be working the next day, and maybe until that particular job would be finished. The job was on the Armagh road, the council were taking a big corner off to make the road a bit straighter. The job was like writing your life story with all the paper work, every load had to be accounted for. Every load that you moved had to be signed for by a ganger man or foreman, and the name of the place where you dumped your load and the time you dumped it, there was a clock in the lorry which had a disc put in it every morning, and every time the lorry stopped it showed up on the disc, I guess it is what they call a tachograph now, back then we didn't know the names of these things, all we knew was that the boss was watching everything we did. If it took you over certain time, you would have to explain why, and our boss Mr Egan always wanted to know all the answers, he always seem to be a bit a bit suspicious of anything you would tell him, and always called every one by their surname. On my first day on this job I had got loaded up by the excavator, the driver was Jimmy McElvanny, always known as big Jimmy. Anyway the weather was very wet, we had to drive in and out of the site over a row of railway sleepers, otherwise you would get bogged down. Jimmy would always give the digger engine a couple of revs to tell you were full, he was a good driver and knew what he was doing. As I was just coming out on the road, Mr Egan arrived, he put his hand up for me to stop, put his foot on the axle of the lorry to inspect the load, "do you call that a full load Sherry", I felt like saying I was christened James, I felt like saying it, and honestly, getting the sack would have suited me fine, but it would not have been the right thing to do, because it would have put John in an awkward spot. Egan jumped down from the lorry, and I went to pull away out of the site, but I was now stuck as I had lost the momentum needed to get out of the site onto the firmer ground. They called another lorry that was waiting, which was driven by John Barber, to give me a pull out, and then he got stuck as well, so that was two lorries stuck, and two more sitting by the roadside waiting, and they could not get in because we were in their way, and all because he wanted me to have what he called a full load. Then Egan just gets into his car and off he goes. Big Jimmy wanted to give us a push out with the excavator, but was told to stay on his own job by the site foreman, what he called his own job was, if there were no lorries waiting Jimmy was push the soil into a big pile, so he could load the lorries that much easier, it was Jimmy's idea in the first place. The foreman wandered off down the site and Jimmy came over and got us pushed out, things always went a bit smoother when he was gone. It wasn't long before I got rid of the old number thirteen and got a nice newer lorry, number twenty-three. I thought this one is nearly too good for me, because I was worried in case anything would happen to it. When John told me about it, he said to take good care of it. By the time I got the new lorry the weather was better and dryer, and we were told that we no longer needed sleepers to get in and out of the site, and that the ground was firm enough to carry the trucks without sleepers. I was the first one to test the new plan. I got loaded up and heard the revving of Jimmy's digger, I started to move off, but the back wheels began to sink and spin, other drivers were shouting at me to give it the "gutty", then I heard a small little click, but did not think it was anything serious, I put my foot on the accelerator, but now the wheels were not moving at all. John barber came over and said he thought it was the half shaft gone, not a good start with my new lorry which I was supposed to take good care of. I was towed into the Yard, and given the old lorry back again. Anyway before the day had gone, the same thing happened to John Barbers lorry, these lorries were Ford VE8's and were very powerful, it seems the were a bit known for this kind of thing. When it happened with John Barber, there had to be something odd about it, John was a good steady driver, then the next day it happened to another good experienced man, Paddy Mc Kenna. After this I didn't feel quite so bad about the whole thing, but I was still finding it hard to get used to it all. I didn't know anyone in Monaghan town, I would not have been there very often, most of my social activities had been in the North. Anyway I always thought to myself, I will never draw my pension here, after a while I got a bit better used it. I know there were lots of people who would give anything to be in this job, I enjoyed it better when I would be sent to Castleblaney, Carrickmacross or Ballybay for a couple of weeks. We would get paid extra, "subsistence", and it made for a bit of a change.

Changing Lanes

After a while I bought myself a car so I could get around a lot more. It was thirteen miles from Monaghan to where my mother lived, and she expected to see me at least once a week, so the car came in handy. It was a big car a black Austen seventy, Henry Ford's favourite colour, it only did about eighteen miles to the gallon. It would be full up with people going to football matches, they all paid their way, and we went to dances all over the place. You could cram an awful lot of people into it, I remember getting 5 people in there, I know with the size of cars today that may not seem a lot, but the cars in those days were not people carriers. The front seat was a bench seat, the gear change was on the steering wheel, called a column shift, it had a radio and a heater the whole works, it was very expensive to run, even without things going wrong. I was leaving my sister Nellie to Monaghan one night, and I had been following a van for some time waiting to get a straight bit of road where I could pass, eventually I found a suitable straight part of a road where I could pass As I was about to pass the van, the van turned across the road in front of me, I could not avoid hitting it. I got out of my car and I asked the driver if there was anyone hurt and, he said there was nobody hurt. I asked why he did such a dangerous thing like that, he said he didn't see me, but I could smell alcohol on him, and his words were a bit slurred. I just didn't know how I was going to handle this, I was three or four miles away from any town, as I have said before, finding a house with a phone in it was not easy in those days, at last a fellow came along in a car, he stopped to see if everyone was alright. I told him that there was nobody hurt. I asked him if would do me a favour and call at the Garda station and ask them to send out a Garda. He said that he was going to Glaslough, and that he would call at the Garda station there and ask them to send someone out and that he would explain to them where the accident took place. It took ages before a Garda arrived, he arrived in the passenger seat of a lorry, he had no bike and was not able to drive, so had no car, it would remind you of some kind of a scene from an old movie like "The Quite Man", but he might as well not to have bothered to turn up, as by the time he arrived the driver had plenty of time to sober up. Even then I don't think he could have walked a straight line! He got taken to court for careless driving but the case was dismissed, so I had to have my car repaired at my own expense and that took the gloss off things for a while.

By this time I had found myself a girlfriend and girlfriends cost money as well. She was the girl I married a few years later her name was Olive Hamill she lived in Monaghan town, her father Gerry was born and bred in Monaghan and likewise all the Hamill family for generations. Her mother came from Dungarvan in County Waterford her name was Mary Morrissey. Gerry was well known in town and the surrounding countryside, he worked for "An Post", the Irish post office, but he was also a very good footballer and played for Monaghan Harps. Sadly Gerry died in 1977 and Mary died a number of years ago, Olive and I got engaged just before Christmas.

Despite some of the setbacks we managed to get around a lot of places, but then trouble began flare up in the middle-east. President Nasser had blocked the Suez Canal so no oil could get through from the Arab oilfields, there was some oil getting through from other places, and from ships sailing the longer route around the southern tip of Africa, but nowhere near enough to meet everybody's needs. There was a big increase in the price of petrol and rumours of drivers being stood off from council jobs. To tell the truth, I was not bothered about what was going to happen, as I had no intention of making this a long term job, in fact it would be a blessing in disguise I would just up and go, and there would no more jobs arranged for me. I had lost three years of good earnings, changing about from job to job, it was all very unsettling, so if it happened, I could leave without upsetting anyone. I was not going to let anyone know that I didn't care about the job. anyway Olive and I decided to get engaged, it was a few days before Christmas, it was almost certain by the look of things that I would be off to England in the new year and get myself a job, and Olive would join me latter in the year. It was only a short time after this I had a letter from the Council stating that I was no longer required after 22nd January 1956. There were lots of things happening around the border at this time, we would sit in the car every night, listening to the sound of gunfire. On one particular night, we were having a game of 45, I won't go into finer points of the game, and there would be maybe eight players at a table, or a second table of eight if you could find the players. Each player would be charged an entry fee to play, but the total winnings would need to be worth at least double the value of what you were playing for, in order to make it worthwhile My mother had a few turkeys that she didn't get sold before Christmas, and the Hamill family said that they would raffle them for her in the card game.

It was 1st January 1957, and people would not have been working on that day, as it was a church holiday. People had started to come early for the game of cards, and they would stand outside having a chat meeting friends. Olive and I were about to get into the car to go, when we heard the rattle of gun fire, this would happen quite often at night in those times, but not as early as this. It was now only 6pm in the evening, so it was some shock when we went into work next morning, to be told that Feargal O'Hanlon had been killed at Brookborough in Fermanagh the night before, during a raid on the R.U.C barracks, this was the gunfire we had heard the night before. I knew Feargal very well, he worked for Monaghan County Council in the drawing office. I would see him about most days, as he lived only a couple doors away from where I was staying with Mary Treanor. He loved the Gaelic football, in the evenings he would sit on the window sill of his own house with a few other lads. One of the lads was Sean South, his comrade who was killed alongside him on that fateful night. I would have lots of chats with Feargal and the lads, the topic would always be football. Monaghan were doing well in the junior championship. I had my own car and could get to all the matches, they went on to win the all-Ireland junior championship against London in Newbridge County Kildare. Anyway, getting back to Feargal O'Hanlon, in the time that I knew him. He was always a nice young lad, and his death was a terrible shock to everyone. I said at the time if I ever have a son I will call him Fergal, and thank God, I have two lovely Sons, and the first one born I called Fergal. The name was quite rare around that time, but I liked the name, and might well have called my son by that name in anyway. Fergal is an ancient Celtic name which means great warrior, and was the name of some of the ancient kings of Ireland. Feargals funeral took place in Monaghan, their remains were brought back from Brookborough, it was the largest funeral ever seen, very emotional all the way through, you would have to say that maybe he saw himself in a similar role as Padraig Pearse, in his diary, found after his death Feargal wrote,

"This might be it, you know neither the time nor the hour, keep cool and pray."

On Christmas day he wrote-

"A good conscience is a continual Christmas",

Whatever was in this young man's mind that night when he left his home, whether he seen himself in the mould of Pearse, he was and is looked upon as a brave Irishman who died for his country.

CHAPTER 20

TIME TO CHANGE

I FINELY DECIDED that this was time to stop changing about from place to place, and from job to job. As I mentioned earlier, I had lost three years of good earnings, from now on I was going to make my own decisions. I have no regrets about it, it was all part of how my life would be shaped for me, I have two lovely sons and a lovely grandson, and I thank God for that, but it took a long time before I could see it like that.

At last things were beginning to happen quite fast, as I said I had the letter from Monaghan County telling that my presence would be no longer required after January 22nd 1957. I was not the only one there were other men as well. It was mainly the single men that were laid off, but single men who had been there for a number of years were not laid off, which was right and proper. We had a Trade Union, for what it was worth, we had a meeting a few weeks before the layoff, as it turned out I was the only fully paid up member, so we would not have much of chance if we wanted to make a fight of it, but it didn't bother me much, I just wanted to get away from it all.

So I was off again to England at the end January, and I got a job a couple days after arriving there, and after a few months, I changed to another job, the money was better, and they supplied transport to and from the job, although it was nearly the last job I might have ever had,

James Sherry

I must have had my mother's prayers looking after me. I was working for a company called Press we were laying a big pipeline from the Isle of Grain to Cobham. The trench was about nine feet wide and seven or eight deep. The pipes were about thirty feet long, and three feet in diameter. The pipes were running alongside each other in the trench, with a bit of space in between them. My job was to attach a long chain with a hook on each end, which would attach to each end of the pipe, it would then be lifted by the crane and lowered into the trench. Everything was going very well, I would always hold the pipe steady until it was over the trench, and ready to be lowered into the trench, to the men who were going to fit the pipes together. I was carrying out the same routine when suddenly there was a big blue flash, I felt as if I was been crushed into a ball by some kind of giant crusher, I thought I was dying, but it was all over in a few seconds. The other lads could not believe it when I scrambled to my feet, I was dazed and in shock, I still didn't know what had happened, when they told that the jib of the crane had caught the overhead electric cables, I thought I must have had someone's prayers. I was wearing hobnail boots at the time, which was not the ideal footwear in a situation like this. I was wearing leather gloves, my fingers on both hands burned, but not too badly thank God- there was 11,000 volts going through these cables. The power was cut off over a big part of the south east region, as it tripped the local substation. It was not long until the people from the electricity Board arrived, they found it hard to believe that no one was killed or seriously injured.

During the time I was working on the pipeline Olive's brother Frank was living in the same house as me, which was my sister Maggie's house in Windsor Road. I had got Frank a job on the pipeline whilst I was working there, and when the pipeline came into Strood and it was continuing on towards Gravesend, the crew had to be cut as there was not the need for as many men then. I was one of the men that was let go, but Frank was lucky enough to stay. I was glad that he was able to stay on as I would have felt bad having taken him to the job in the first place.

Changing Lanes

I went back to Ireland in July as planned, Olive my girl came back to England with me, then not long after that I was made redundant again, this was not a good time of year to be out of work as winter was not far away. I was thinking of looking for a job in a factory to tide me through the winter, then something else came into my head. Not far from where I had been working on the pipeline there was a little Oil Refinery it was called Berry Wiggins, I thought I would give it a try.

CHAPTER 21

A HAPPY JOB

I ARRIVED AT Berry Wiggins and I asked at the gate house if there were any job vacancies, the man at the gate said he thought there might be and he directed me towards an office where I would meet a man called Mr Wellard. The gateman said that he would phone the office and tell him that I was on my way over. Mr Wellard was a very pleasant and friendly man, I felt very comfortable and very much at ease. He said I believe you are looking for a job, he asked his secretary, who was also his daughter, to make a cup of tea, he went on to ask me what kind of work I did in my last job and the reason for leaving. I told that I had been working on a pipe line and that my job was called as a slinger or rigger, I didn't know it at the time, but my answer was spot on. Then he asked my reason for leaving, I said that the job had finished and that I had been made redundant. He seemed satisfied with what I told him, then he told that they were looking people to work in the rigging gang. Then he asked me if I had a good head for heights, when I told him that I was not afraid of heights, he said that I seemed to be the kind of person they were looking for. He told me what the weekly wages and the starting times were, and all the conditions of employment, and asked me if I was happy with all that, I said I was, and he asked when I wanted to start, I said as soon as possible, he said, "you can start tomorrow morning".

Changing Lanes

I met the gang the next morning and hit it off straight away. There was a happy relaxed feeling about everything, Vic Blondage our foreman was waiting for me at the gate the next morning. He talked to me like a father, he was a great rigger and a gentleman. He knew his rigging inside out, I just could not believe my luck, the flat rate was nearly as much as I was getting on my last job with overtime included, it was a dream job. The work was very interesting and always a bit of a challenge. It was a small little refinery, cranes were out of the question. We used all old style lifting gear, we would use steel barge poles for lifting whatever needing lifting. We would fix a large pulley block to the pole, and then we would fix guide wires to the pole, which would keep in position when raised to an upright position by a winch. The guide wires would be fixed to something secure, usually heavy metal stakes driven into the ground by means of fourteen pound hammer. The winch would have to be fixed in a similar way, we would fix a lifting block to a nearby steel structure, and then the wire from the winch would be treaded through the lifting block and onto the barge pole, which then would be lifted into an upright position. The guide wires would then be fixed to the stakes. Then the same procedure would be used on another pole, you would always need two poles, one each side of whatever you were lifting. Sometimes we used steel derricks for lifting the real heavy stuff, such as tall metal chimney stacks. The derrick could be extended to whatever height you needed by bolting extra sections together. A Bosun's chair would have to be fixed to the derricks in order that someone could go up and release the slings from whatever you were lifting. Sometimes we would have to move tanks from one place to another, we would get some lengths of pipe about six inches in diameter, and lay them out about two foot apart. Then get some railway sleepers, and lay them on top of the pipes. The pipes could now be used as rollers. The sleepers would be fixed together with metal cleeks, then we would have to jack the tank up, and push the platform, or cradle as it was usually called. It was all very interesting work, we did lots of scaffolding as well, I loved every bit of it, they were a great bunch of lads. Then my brother Felix came to Gillingham looking for a job, I had a word with the foreman and he got a job along with me, I was delighted, and I am sure it was the best job he ever had, I thought he would be there for years to come, but it turned out to be months rather than years, he went to Ireland for Christmas, and never came back to us, when he came back to England he went to London to work. The foreman had great time for him, he would often say to me, if your brother ever wants to come back there will always be a job for him.

Things were beginning change around the time Felix left, there was a man working on the site who belonged to a different union from us, he belonged to the Construction Engineering Union, we were in the Transport and General Workers Union, which catered more for drivers and labourers. He advised us to transfer to the Construction Engineering Union, it was a union that catered better for our kind of work. So we joined the CEU as it was better known, we got a bit of flak from the Transport and General Workers Union, but we were at last recognized as qualified trades' men. We got a good increase in our wages, we did some unbelievable jobs without hardly any motorized assistance. The company had their own railway line through the refinery, we transported tanks and other large objects on our quickly assembled trolley and rollers. I only wish we had the video cameras then that we have today. I must say I enjoyed every minute of it, I don't think I ever had a miserable day while I worked there, then after a while I was elected shop steward. I have to say it changed things a little, I felt a bit more isolated, there were always going to be confrontations from somewhere or other. Your first duty was to look after your members at all times, and sometimes you would find yourself having to discipline one of your own members, or give a bit advice if they were out of order. I have to say I had a good relationship with my members, I would always keep them well informed, and I had a fair and sensible relationship with the management. I attended my union branch once a month to pay in my union member's money. I got elected onto the branch committee, on which I gained a lot experience, and from that I got to be good friends with a lot of people there, Dave Savage was one in particular. He had lots of contacts, he would be on the lookout for any good jobs that were going. He found out that there was a vacancy for a scaffolder at the BP refinery on the Isle of Grain. He told me I should apply for it straight away, he told me what the hourly rate was, he knew most of the conditions of the job, and it all sounded great. I should have been over the moon about it, it's hard to believe but somehow I wished I not heard about it. From the day I started there I said to myself I will never leave this job, I thought about all the good friends I had there. Not long after I started on Berry Wiggins I had an awful accident on my way home from work. I broke both my legs in a number of places, I still have a metal plate in my leg, and I had a fractured skull, and was in Gravesend Hospital for 16 weeks. For the first few weeks in hospital it was touch and go. The lads were all very kind to me, they came to visit me in hospital, and they took up a collection for me. I was out of work for over six months and I was very grateful for everything they did for me. The NHS sick benefit at that time was £2. 04s per week, and after a number of weeks, it went down to half, and then to nothing. When I went back to work, I was not able to do heavy work for a while, the lads helped me a lot, and the company paid me full pay. So it's easy to understand why I didn't want to leave. I asked for a lot of people's opinion, and everyone said go for it. I went for my interview, and obviously must have impressed the board, I passed my medical, and I had a great reference from Mr John Wellard, the Berry Wiggins Refinery manager.

 I have to say I was not looking forward to starting my new job, I had no worries about being able to do the job, I had spent six years working with a good bunch of lads, I just wondered what it would be like. But I need not have worried, it might have been the other way round, Dave Savage had been talking to the boys, and had built up a big reputation for me that I could have done without. Dave had told them that I was a very strong no nonsense union man, I think they were waiting for this wild man to break out, sure I knew the union rules, but I didn't go around shouting about it, they found out that I was quieter than most, but I never let anyone lead me astray. Some of the lads had the habit of going into the "hot" changing rooms too early, and getting caught, for which they would have time deducted from them, after a while these lads left and started their own little scaffolding company. BP had only a small crew of scaffolders at the time, whilst Vange Scaffolding had a big crew of scaffolders on the site. We all integrated when required, the BP crew were used mostly for emergencies, but our crew had the first choice when it came to over-time, it didn't take me very long to settle in, and I was glad that I made the move when I did, we were the highest earners on the site, we would always be first on the job to erect the scaffold, and the last there to dismantle the scaffold when the job was finished. Sometimes this would lead to overtime, I think we were the envy of the refinery, all the trades were the same rate of pay, but we got more overtime than any of the other trades because we were always in demand. All the trades got extra money if they had to work under certain conditions, such as inside tanks or vessels, anything like this, it would come under the category of confined space, then if it was particularly dirty inside whatever you were working, it would come under the wording of dirt and confined space. Sometimes you might be required to wear an air-line and mask because the environment was toxic to breath, which added more to your to your condition money. Then there was height money, this came into effect when you went above a certain height above ground. We had great working conditions, you were allowed in early to the amenities to have a shower if you were working in any of the conditions mentioned above, we had a good negotiating committee of shop stewards, and they would need to be. Around this time there were signs on the horizon that the government were considering bringing in a policy of wage restraint, advocating for the unions to look at ways of relaxing some of the working regulations, this looked like a dangerous road to think about going down, however the full time union officials decided to have a look at what possibilities there might be. We knew the Government was going to impose a strict wage restraint, so we reluctantly agreed to allow some limited talks to begin.

I suppose it was understandable that the talks were allowed to take place, there were some trades who got very little over-time, they were hoping to find some ways of improving their take home pay, because of the demand for scaffolders we got more over-time than any other trade, which meant a big difference in our take home pay and some of the other trades. One of the proposals the Company had on this new document, was that there would no payment for working over-time, we would get time in-lieu instead, the company knew this would appeal more to the trades who didn't work much over-time, other proposals, such as conditions payments for heights, dirt and confined space, payment for these items would cease. Then the next plan was the relaxing of some demarcations, this meant that different trades could integrate and work on certain jobs, previously only a scaffolder could alter scaffold, or a fitter undo a bolt on a pipe etc, but what was now being planned, was that as long as the trade that was the established trade had at least fifty percent of the work force on that job, then other "non-qualified" workers would be able to do the same jobs. Scaffolders were the only trade not affected by changes in the demarcations, because of the nature of the job none of the other trades wanted to touch scaffolding.

Some of us never thought it would ever reach the negotiating table, and after long drawn out discussions, an agreement was reached. We had been led to believe, that unless all the unions agreed, there could be no changes to the working agreement. The members of the boilermakers union rejected the agreement, but were then told by their full time officials, that because it was going to benefit the biggest majority of workers on the site, that the full time officials could sign the agreement, whether the members liked it or not, and sign it they did. We got a good increase on our weekly basic pay and holiday pay, but a lot of us were going to be a lot worse off. The company agreed to pay us another payment of twenty five pounds in six months after the agreement was signed, the agreement was signed near the end of March. Then came the budget day in the first week of April, and the Government brought in a strict wage restraint, no wage increase for at least a year, so that meant come September, we would not be able to get our twenty five pounds. Up until now the unions and the company had a very good working relationship, but now a lot of discontent had set in, we had given up nearly everything, yet the process workers were not trades men, and the had not given up anything, but they would get a per cent of our wage, some of these things came back to haunt us a few years later.

The process workers had a different way of negotiation to ours, they had a number of different grades, grade A was top grade, and B the next lower grade, and so on In my early days at BP I not been much involved in the official role, if either of our shop Stewards were not available I would stand in their place, and when one of them decided he didn't want to do the job anymore, my name was put forward and I got elected. There were lots of troublesome times ahead of us, we didn't have much bargaining power left negotiating had become very limited, but somehow we always managed to come up with ideas of how to get increases in our wages, of course every item had to be vetted by the department of employment to make sure it was genuine before we got any increase.

Sometime later the process workers were having negotiations with the company but the talks broke down. The process workers belonged to the transport and general workers union, they were threatening strike action. They asked us not to do any of their work whilst they were out on strike, of course we told them we would not dream of touching their work. After a short time the Company asked them to lift their strike threat and they would have discussions about it, everything about it was kept very quiet. When our unions negotiated an agreement with the company, the process workers would always know what was in the agreement. We had had an agreement with the company that the process workers would go never go above our rate pay, but it's hard to keep things a secret for very long, we had our suspicions that there was something being kept back from us.

What happened was, they had their grade A men made up to supervisors, and the grade B men made up to grade A, and so on. The tradesmen had always been at the top of the wage bracket, now we could take industrial action if there was a no agreement reached. The company were saying that they had the right to make these men up to supervisors, it seemed to us like a change of heart,

Changing Lanes

because it was part of the deal we signed a few years previous, that the company would get rid of supervisors or charge hands as they were called, but they were still one and the same. We were all of the opinion that the company did not think that we would take strike action, but they were very much mistaken, because on the twenty first of October nineteen seventy four, that was exactly what we did. It was a mighty big decision, but we had very few options, we felt we were being demoted to grade B tradesmen, the process workers had not made any concessions, while we, the craft tradesmen had given almost everything up. The company denied that there was ever a deal made with the process workers, right up until the afternoon of the day before the strike. We had set the date, and what options we had left, we didn't know if we could win, or for how long it would last. We had organized round the clock picketing of the entrance to the oil refinery, blocking the road in and out. A lot of people did not have their own cars, so we tried working it out that there would be a few cars on each shift to give lifts to people who didn't have cars. There were eleven shop stewards, and we always wanted to have at least one shop steward on each shift. I did not have a car, so I opted for the days that I knew I would have a better chance of getting a lift. The day was from twelve noon until six in the afternoon, it was the hardest shift, because it was the time of day that the majority tankers, and any other type of transport would be arriving to go into the refinery, on the first day we had a great turnout of support, it was very encouraging.

We also heard some news on that day that was less encouraging. We had asked the foremen not to do any of our work, but then we heard that the foreman had had a meeting, and a few had decided that they would do our work. I think at first there was only one who was willing to do our work, but the rest decided to follow suit a bit later. We had warned the foremen that would not cooperate with them, if or when we got back to work, now the foremen were named as scabs, so they got a roasting everyday going to and from work, we did not want any violence, but sometimes it came close to it, as their cars would be rocked from side to side. It must have been a very scary experience for them, running the gauntlet every morning and afternoon, but there was always a big police presence there waiting for an opportunity to arrest someone. We had a source in which we could feed false information back to the police, maybe we would "leak" it, that we were going to have an extra big demo, and the place would packed with police, this worked well for us as when the lorries tried to run us off the road by driving straight at us, when there was a large police presence the drivers would think twice. As time went on there was a bit of a drop in numbers on the picket line, it was not the lack of enthusiasm for the strike, but getting out there was quite a problem, the refinery was about twenty miles from the Medway towns, and transport was a bit limited. There were some of the lads getting bits of work from time to time, the union officials agreed that we could do this, I did this myself now and then, but always arranged for someone to do my picket duty for me. Getting back to getting a lift, one day I could not manage to get a lift, so I caught the train to Strood and started walking from there, I got as far as the Windmill pub when a tanker came along, he pulled up and asked if I wanted lift, I asked him where he was going, and he said he was going to the Isle of Grain, I said that will do for me, I got in and we chatted away about different things until we got closer to the Refinery and there was there was a tail back of traffic, and he asked what is going on here, I told him that there was a strike on, he asked what is it was all about, I told him it is too long a story and I didn't have enough time to explain, I told him that I was one of shop the stewards and that I am was going to join the picket line, and that I would be asking him not to cross the picket line, he asked and if he did cross the line what would happen, I said so far nobody has crossed the line, and to remember he had to come out again, all I could say it could be a nasty experience, and that there may or may not be a police presence. I told him that there is a pub right beside the picket line, and that there was a payphone in there which he could use to ring his employer to tell him the position, I told him, "I will go in along with you and talk to your boss if you want me to, but I'm sorry, but I have to go now, you can make your way towards the picket line, which you would have done if, you had not met up with me, many thanks for the lift". He was a nice fellow, and I didn't feel good about what I had done, but in desperate times sometimes you have to do unpleasant things, but on the whole we were pretty well behaved. Most of the time there was a big Police presence, and sometimes overdoing their duty. One particular time I remember, when a few men were doing some of the tradesmen's work, and a young girl from the local newspaper went to take a picture of it, a police Sergeant stood out in front of her and opened his overcoat so she didn't get a picture, she told us afterwards that it didn't make much difference, as they would not have published it anyway. None of the papers gave us any publicity, but I sure they would have done if we had been misbehaving.

It was wintertime, and not the best time of the year to be on strike, we had no shelter, no heat, or any way to boil a kettle for a cup of tea. We could not make any arrangements before the strike, because we didn't know if there was going to be a strike, anyway we organized some scaffolding and a tarpaulin, and we erected a little shelter for ourselves. We gathered up some wood and got ourselves some coal, so this was a big help. We got an old forty gallon oil drum and punched some holes in it, we put the wood and some coal into it and some paraffin and got a fire going, then later on, we got a brazier, which was more economic than the oil drum and was a lot cleaner, it gave the boys on night picket a bit more comfort, but there would rarely be much activity during the night watch, the day watch was the worst. It was from twelve noon to six pm, there would always be a big police presence during the day, but now they were beginning to get a bit tougher with us. From the beginning of the strike, the shop steward always stand out on the road and put his hand out to slow the vehicles to a stop. It was a bit scary at times as some of the drivers would not slow down until they nearly touched you. I suppose you could call it playing chicken. Then one day when I stopped a vehicle a Police Officer came over to me and warned me if I did it again that he would arrest me, I had already been doing this for weeks, and had not been warned before. Anyway we all had quick chat about what had happened, they were a great bunch of lads, they all agreed that they would stand out alongside me, and see then what he would do, and he could not arrest me without arresting all the rest of the lads. When the next vehicle drove towards us we all stepped out together, he didn't do anything about it, but a few minutes later he came over to me and said, "if you are on this picket tomorrow, I will arrest you", I asked him why he was going to arrest me, he gave me a very angry look, and he looked right into my face and said, "you know why", I said no I didn't know why, and he repeated the same words a number of times, it was 22nd November 1974, the night after the Birmingham pub bombings, I thought that maybe that might have something to do with it, as I had an Irish accent, most of the lads thought it could have had something to do with it. The next day a few of our shop stewards, along with some of the top union officials went to number eleven Downing Street to meet with Merlyn Reese and ask for better police behaviour and it did improve, but there would always be bits of trouble breaking out from time to time.

As the time went on things were looking a bit bleak, there was trouble out in the middle East, and oil was not as easy to come by, and there was also a bit of a recession, it looked as if we were in for a long battle. We agreed amongst ourselves that if anyone could get a bit of work anywhere, it would be OK to take it, as long as we had enough people to manage the picket line. I had a few Irish connections, and managed to get a bit of work for myself and a few of the lads, which myself and the lads were grateful for, Christmas was drawing near, and I was going to do my utmost to make sure my family did not suffer, and sure enough the man I worked for, arrived at my home a few nights before Christmas with a nice bit of money for me, his name was the Pat Clifford, who sadly has passed away a few years ago, God bless him, I could tell he got as much joy out of it as I did, so the family had a decent Christmas after all. But all too soon Christmas was over, but nothing had changed, there were appearing little rumbles of discontent from a few of the lads, but only a small few, asking us when were we going to get them back to work, there was not a lot we could say to them, only that we did warn them when we took the vote to take strike action, that it could be a long battle, and that there was a risk that we might not win, it was difficult now, but we had to stand firm and keep trying every avenue possible. We decided to picket BP Company House in London, we knew that BP did not like publicity as regards strike action, we had tried all the newspapers and none of them wanted to know, because they were afraid of losing their revenue on their BP adverts. We hired some coaches, and we got a good response from the lads, but left enough to man the picket lines, this was new ground to us, so we didn't know what to expect, we were well received, we were invited inside in little groups and treated to some refreshments, we got the impression that the management at the Isle Of Grain were economic with the truth, we got together the next day and decided to up the tempo on the foremen going to and from work and keep it up for as long as it took. We had effigies of scab foremen hanging from whatever we could hooked them onto, then we got in touch with the shop stewards on Isle of Grain power station, to ask them to give us some support, and they agreed whole heartily. Big Bill Thompson was the man to get it all organized, and no better man. They arrived at about 0730 on a Friday in full strength, there were traffic jams all the way back to Strood, and the same again the next week. It was bigger and more disruptive, the public were getting angry now about all the disruptions on the roads, and of course BP did not like bad publicity, however it brought a breakthrough from an independent body, it was Department of Employment who decided to try to break the deadlock and get discussions started. I think this was a relief to both sides. We had stood firm always, all the way, it was a bit nerve wrecking at times, there were a few who would be asking us when were we going to get them back to work, all you could do was to remind them, that they voted for the strike, and they knew from the beginning that it could take a long time and might not be easy.

    The talks got started and continued for a number of days, until at last we reached an agreement, we didn't get everything we asked for, but then we didn't expect to, the most important thing was getting parity back with grade A operators. The company had it written into the new agreement that there would be no animosity from the craftsmen towards anyone who worked on any of the craftmen's jobs. The road back was not going to be smooth, the company had been telling us that the reason they made the grade B operators up to the craftsmen's rate, was they were self-supervised, in reality we were in the same position, nobody told us how to do the job, the foreman would show us the job that needed doing and we got on and done it. I was employed as a scaffolder and our foreman was never a scaffolder, so how could he supervise us, in normal conditions we would sort out what material we needed for that particular job, we would then phone Vange, who was the scaffolding contractor on the Refinery, and ask them to send out the material we needed. Once we went back to work things changed around a bit, as the company were saying that we were not self-supervised. We had been out on strike from 21st October '74, until 21st January '75, it was a terrible atmosphere on our first day back, and it lasted for quite some time, in fact some of the men never really got it out of their system. Most of us did not enjoy what we were doing, how we were treating the foremen, as the majority of the foremen were good decent men to work for, but they were put in an awkward position, they now were telling men how to do jobs, that some of the foremen had no idea how to do. But there were a lot of angry men around who thought that these, "scabs", as they were called, needed to be taught a lesson in-case anything similar happened in the future. Anyhow things did settle down eventually, as they say time is a great healer. A few years later some changes came about regarding the BP Scaffolding crews, the company approached John Ogilvy and myself, as we were the two shop stewards who represented the Construction Union, they wanted to know what the scaffolding crews would feel if they were offered voluntary redundancy with a decent pay out, they said they were just putting out feelers, they said if no one was interested that would be the end of it, they also said it would have to be unanimous. BP said they didn't want anyone to be pressurised in anyway, they also said they would guarantee a job with Vange Scaffolding for as long as we wanted it. I had quite an open mind about it, I had a longer time served than anyone else, and I would have the most to gain, the closer one got to retiring the less the less pay-out you would get, and our retiring age was sixty. So after a lot of thought, inwardly I made my mind up to go for it without telling anyone how I felt about it. All the men were all in favour of it except one, who was a bit unsure, he was a good friend of mine I gave him time to think about it, without letting him know what I was going to do. He finally decided to go for it, it was a big decision for all of us, the only thing we would lose out on, was our sick pay, and that didn't bother me at all. But a lot of our lads were bad timekeepers. I think that this was one of the reasons which led to the company to come up with idea, there had been times when I was the only scaffolder present, and I was the shop steward. The way I saw it, I was going to be better off, Vange Scaffolding supplied free transport to and from Grain, so we didn't have to worry how we were going to get there, we were also allowed to use the BP canteen and enjoy all the privileges we had before, to me there was no upheaval at all.

It was quite a smooth change over, and I hardly needed time to settle in after all I had been working here for years. I have to say I enjoyed my time there, we changed over on the first week in November '78, I walked out of the gates on Friday employed by BP, and back in on Monday morning to work for Vange. The first thing I did when I received the pay-out was to pay my mortgage off and clear all the other debts that I had, it was a great feeling to be free of the worry of them, but sorry to say the good feeling was short lived, my marriage broke up in January '79. I found it very hard to tell anyone about it, even my own family, I wanted to make sure that my mother who was living back in Ireland would never know about it.

Mum never did get to know about it, and sadly she died a few months later in May '79. I had already pricked up enough courage to tell my sister Cassie who lived on the Isle of Wight with her husband Winfred, they were great to me. As I said earlier, my sister was a nurse, she was now retired, and her husband was a retired surgeon. Cassie broke the news to the rest of the family, so they knew by the time I got home for my mother's funeral. The company I was working for were good to me, even though I had only been working there for a few months, they gave me time off with pay for the bereavement, the fellow in charge of the job, his name was Kitch Perkins was very good to me, if I needed time off to go and see a Solicitor or anything like that, he never stopped any time from my wages. We had worked together when he was working as a scaffolder on other jobs, and this bit of kindness helped to make life a bit easier.

I needed to try and make life as comfortable as I could for my two boys and myself, and so I decided to buy myself a car sometime later on in the year, but first I needed to take driving lessons. I had a Northern Ireland licence but had let it run too long without renewing it, so I needed to take my driving test again. We wanted to go to Ireland on holiday about the last week in July, it was all a bit tricky. I could not buy a car in case I didn't pass my driving test, so we decided we would book our holiday, car or no car, we just hoped and prayed for the best. I was really worried that I would let the boys down. I had lot of changes of driving instructors, which didn't help, then I got a young fellow with me for the last few lessons, when I saw him the first time, I thought this is all that I need, but it turned out he was the best of the whole lot. I thought what a pity I didn't have him from the start, he gave me a lot of confidence he told me lots of simple things, but important things. I told him I had failed the test once before. He asked me if I knew what I failed on, I told him that it was failing to make proper progress in traffic, in other words I waited too long at the junction of a main road before pulling out onto the main road, there was a car approaching towards me and I thought it was a bit risky, some of the other instructors were telling me, if in doubt- don't pull out. "Well", he said, "most times you would get away it, it's a hard one". The test was to be in Gravesend, a town I didn't know much about. He told me there was no reason why I shouldn't pass, just keep my full concentration for twenty minutes or a half an hour at the most.

Anyway the dreaded day arrived and off we went, it was a very hot morning and sweat was running off me. I seemed to be doing alright, then as I approached a roundabout a big car drove straight across in front of me, I stepped on the brakes and stopped, the other car was approaching from my left, he was in the wrong, but I just could not convince myself that I had done nothing wrong, but I was a bit more nervous from that point in, but I thought, whatever the outcome I would be glad when it was all over, but not as glad as I was when he said, "I am pleased to tell you Mr Sherry you have passed your driving test", I just felt on top of the world, not so much for myself but for the two boys. This was going to make a big difference in our lives, our holiday was only week away, but we could book a hire car at Belfast Airport for our holiday. I could not wait to get home and tell the boys the good news. When I got home I could not resist having a little joke with them, when they asked me if I passed, I said I am sorry I failed, the looks on their faces said it all, but the looks on their faces soon changed when I told them that I had passed, they said they had been down at the church all morning praying and lighting candles for me, I said that's what had done it for us. I said we will go around to Browns travel agents, which was only about a hundred yards away, this was where we booked nearly all our holidays, they knew us quite well, and they were always very helpful, we got all booked and everything sorted very quickly.

Off we went on the train to London, travelling home was a lot different then, you would get a train to London Victoria, change there and get the underground to Gloucester road underground station, from there it was only a short distance to walk to the bus terminal at the Tara Hotel, which brought you to Heathrow Airport. The boys were very excited about it all, it was a new venture for us all, I was a bit more worried than exited, as I had never driven on a motorway before, but Fergal my eldest son got himself well read up on the maps and motorways, and we decided he would do the navigations. We picked our hire car up at Belfast airport, a nice green coloured Vauxhall Chevrolet "NIA 2225", the two boys would still be able to tell you that number to this day, and we headed off towards Aughnacloy. After all this travel and changing, it was just now a couple of miles from home that we had our first set back. When we got to Moy Bridge there was a hijacked lorry blocking the road on the Tyrone side of the border, we had to turn around and find another crossing at Caledon, it was all part of the fun for the lads. We arrived safe at our destination, all well pleased with ourselves, for the first time we had own transport, we could go wherever we wanted to for the first time ever, and it was a great feeling. For many years my brother Arthur and his wife Mary and their two children would come to Ireland at around this time. Derrick and Brenda would be playing in the all-Ireland Fleadh Cheoil music festival every year around this time, we didn't go very far till after they arrived, we wanted to see them before we went off on our mini tour. We went off to the west of Ireland, the boys had never been to any other part of Ireland except Monaghan before now. So far it was the best holiday we had ever had, for the first time there were no restrictions on us from anyone, no "why don't you do that..?", or "why didn't you do this…?", "or I don't want to go there…", no worrying about what clothes we had to wear, no worries about "looking good", we did what all three of US wanted to, for the first time ever. Sometimes people mean well, but it's not always what you want, or what's best, we were just enjoying to the full every day, even when the weather would not be so good, we would find some amusements indoors. We had decided that we would go back to Dromore in about a week's time, my brother Felix would be holding a big dance for the local athletic club, the Glaslough Harriers, a club which he had started his running with many years before and was still very involved in. There would be a big band engaged to play there, and my sister-in-law Mary Connelly, Arthur's wife, would sing along with them. This would be held in the Emyvale Inn, it would always be great night it would be packed out. Anyway on our way back to Monaghan, we decided to make our way back through Bundoran. We pulled into a big hotel at the top of the town, it was called O'Gorman's, we went in and got booked in. It was a lovely place, lovely food, and a big saloon/singing bar, and a big room where the young ones could play pool or lots of other games, or the older children could come into the bar, if they wanted to, provided you kept them under control. The two boys and myself made our way back to Monaghan the next day, wherever we went we had lots of fun, we covered a lot of ground during that four week holiday, but the time seemed to fly, and nobody was looking forward to going back to England. I gave them a bit of comfort by telling them that I would buy a car when I would get back and settled in, then we would be able to go lots of places, and this cheered them up no end. I asked a good friend of mine, his name was Mick Daly, we played music together in the old Brompton Irish club for a few years as part of a little band. I asked him if he could find me a nice little car around £2,000, this was in 1979, and you would get quite a decent little car at that kind of money. It took a little while before he found one that I liked, and by I, I mean of course, one that the boys liked. At last he found one we all liked, it was a 1978 Ford Escort with quite a low mileage. The price was £1,700, it was a lovely colour, it was a kind of between yellow and orange colour, with a black vinyl roof, four doors and boot of course. I was still living in the matrimonial home, and I didn't have a garage, and so far I not been able to find suitable accommodation to move to. I was a bit worried parking the car as it was a very eye catching car, and I was afraid of it getting damaged, so now I was on the lookout for a garage to put it in. Eventually I found a garage, but not before I had some damage done. It cost me quite a bit of money to have it repaired.

At last I found accommodation, it was not top class, but it was a place to lay my head. It was just one room, I shared the kitchen, bathroom and toilet. I was lucky I was working for a good company, and that I could have a shower every afternoon before I came home. I had my own TV and radiocassette player so I could play some tapes. I was always on the lookout for something better, I always needed to be convenient to where I got picked up by my transport for work, but I was happy enough, at least I could please myself what I did. I had lived in rough digs before over the years a few times, so nothing would surprise me. Saturday night would usually be the worst night, there were a few young lads in the house in rooms like myself, and some of their friends would come round and have a drink or possibly taking drugs with them, I came in one Saturday night, and there were three or four of them hoping on all fours and barking like dogs. I don't think that they were bad lads, sometimes they would apologise in the morning, but I always kept my door well locked and bolted in case they made a mistake as to which door was theirs. My own two Boys would come in to see me every evening after school, they were only about ten minute's walk from where I lived. I would take them out somewhere on weekends we were all enjoying ourselves and the boys were counting the months and weeks until holiday time again. Eventually it came round again, and we had another terrific holiday, they were just getting better, I wish we could relive them all again. It was our aim to go to every county in Ireland and we had now reached our goal. It was so good to always have something good to look forward to, but these few years just flew past, then as we were just beginning to talk about and plan the next year's holiday, Mick Daly told me had another nice car, and he thought I might like it. He said he would take me up to have a look at it, he said it would be around the two thousand mark it was a W reg, (I'm sure the boys could tell you the reg of this one too), a lovely Blue coloured Ford Escort Mark 2, top of the range. It was now near the end of the year 1980, but it had only five hundred miles on the clock, we loved the car we had. I said I would like the boys to see it before I made any decision, as much as they loved they car we had, when they saw this one, they could not get it home quick enough, now they really had they car they wanted. As it was mid-winter now we were a bit restricted to travelling about, we were all looking forward to the bright evenings and the summer time, when we would be off home again, and I was just as excited as they were, I just loved to see them happy. Eventually holiday time arrived again, the car was loaded up with everything we might need for the months holiday, and we headed off in the late morning, to drive to the boat from Liverpool, so as to give ourselves plenty of time, and so we could stop and get something to eat and rest. Our boat didn't sail until about nine p.m., we always booked a berth so we could have a good night's rest, and the boat would get in about seven a.m. the next morning, anyway we got there safe and sound everything was going well so far. We would always have a good selection of tapes in the car which we could listen to as we went on our way, we all had much the same taste in music, so we never had any problems. Whilst we were driving along we had been playing some tapes and I asked my navigator to turn on the radio for the news. After a few minutes the news person announced that, Margaret Thatcher had today announced in parliament that British Petroleum were closing their oil refinery on the Isle Of Grain in Kent, I just could not believe what I heard, I was lost for words, I said nothing, I thought, "did I get that right? Did he just say what I think he said?", then the boys said, "Dad, did you hear that?" I said, "I did, but it has only sunk in now". They were only young, but the understood the position right well. I said, "don't worry, I will another job somewhere", somehow I don't think that I quelled their fears, I think they were adult enough to know what the situation on getting jobs were. I said, "listen boys, this is not going to spoil our holiday", I said there was a fellow who had worked on the same job as me, and he had told me to look him up on a job that was just starting in Limerick. I was not kidding them, I said, "after a few days' rest, that's where we'll be heading for, we can see a bit more of the South", and after a few days that's where we went.

    I have often found, if you are looking for a job, the pub can be the best place to go. We got down there in the afternoon, had a wash and a bite to eat, found a pub with a bit of music. I got talking to a fellow about the job that I had in mind, he asked me what I did, and I said was a scaffolder. He said that he thought that they were taking on Scaffolders at the moment, he was a very nice helpful young man, he said he was a welder and he been in Ireland for the past two years on different jobs. He had not been very long on this job, he told me how to get there and wished good luck. I told the boys that things seem to be looking up, but I spoke too soon they would not let me onto the site when we drove out there, they told me that I needed a letter of introduction from someone. Nobody seemed to know who the somebody was, these were troublesome times around home, and in Northern Ireland, this was the summer of 1981, the time of the Hunger Strikes. There were little groups set up throughout the Republic, asking you to beep your horn if you supported the men in the blocks. Anyway I was disappointed that things hadn't gone better, never-the-less we still had a great holiday and got around to lots of places.

Our time at home was soon up and it was time to go back to England, this was always the worst bit, but unusually, I was itching to find out for myself what the situation on the Grain was. I was hoping to get Christmas out of it at least, it was almost September now. When we got back we found out it was closing at the end of the year, in the second week in January 1982. I always remember the Queens words when she officially opened the oil refinery in 1955, when she said, "there will be jobs here for you, your children, and your children's children, but then Maggie Thatcher came along, and in 1982 closed it, or caused it to be closed. She said she wanted a slimmer and fitter work force throughout industry, and she certainly got the slimmer bit right. It was a very sad day for everyone concerned, it was a big part of my life, it was not only losing a good job, it was losing lots good friends as well.

These were not pleasant times, nothing much was happening on the matrimonial side either, one side as bad as the other. The solicitors crossing their T's and doting their I's, it kept dragging on and on. I went to the job centre every day, but could never find anything good. I had a friend who told me that they were looking for Scaffolders on a job in Scotland near Aberdeen, he gave me the name and address of the place as well. They had a notice up on the board stating that people who were willing to travel to seek work, that their travel expenses would be paid, so people could travel to where the jobs were on offer. Now there were no special places mentioned on the board, I went in to the job centre and went up to the desk, I said that I had reliable information about jobs up near Aberdeen, and I said I would be willing to travel there provided that my expenses were paid, the young lady asked me if I had a letter from an employer to say that was a job available for me, or did I have an interview. I said no I did not have an interview, I said I had reliable information, that they were crying out for scaffolders and that I had the right credentials for any kind of scaffolding job, and that I had the confidence that there were there jobs there, she said, "oh no, that's not good enough, you must have proof that there is a job there for you", so I went over and took the notice off the board, and brought over to her, I said can you see any of things that you have just told me on there, I am not an aggressive person, but it was getting to me, I said, "I'm sure it's probably not your fault, but that is misleading rubbish that is on that card", I threw it into the rubbish bin and said that's where it belongs, I said, "I came here for help, but common-sense does not prevail", so I just walked out. After a few months hanging about, Jim Byrnes a local building contractor gave me job which I was very grateful for, it gave me a great lift. I had known Jim for a long time, I knew him before he started his own business, I missed not being able to take the boys on holiday, they were good lads they understood my position. Unfortunately, I had a problem with a hernia which I had kept putting off having an operation for, and towards the end of the year, the doctor told me that I would have to have it done, and that after the operation I would need to have at least 3 months off work. I told Jim what the position was, he very good about it all, he just said come back when you're ready. Sometime later my sister Cassie, who lived on the Isle of Wight with her husband Winfred, asked me to come down to stay with them for a while, I was glad to get the offer, it turned out to be the best thing I had done in a long time. Winfred was a doctor before he retired, he was a surgeon, but also had a qualification as a psychiatrist. One day we got to talking and he asked me how I felt, I said I felt a bit down. I said sometimes I burst into tears, but never in front of anyone, then I feel ashamed of myself, I said I had lots of hard things happen to me before, but I never felt like this. He said, "You are suffering from depression". He asked me to give him the name and address of my GP, and he said he would write to him and explain to him what he thought was wrong with me. My doctor wrote to me and asked me to come in and see him, he said he was going to refer me to a psychiatrist who had his surgery just a short distance away in Rochester. I got an appointment and went to see him, he was a lovely pleasant man. He said just relax and go back as far back as you can remember, he understood the things I told him, and what really poor families had suffered in those days, he was Irish himself, so I am sure he would have seen or heard of the hardships that poor families had to suffer. I told him that my sister had asked my brother, who lived over in New York with his wife Mary and family, if I could go over and stay for a few weeks with them, and they said they would be delighted to have me stay with them, they had just bought a big house and needed an awful of doing to it. He just looked at me and said, "I was going to suggest something similar or whatever you could afford, I am sure this will work wonders Another thing I am going to say to you, from what you have just told me, you have a great story there, why don't you write a book", and he said to me to promise that I would, and I said I would, but I never thought it would take this long to get to where I am now and I haven't finished yet.

My brother Arthur rang me to see when I was thinking of going over, he said himself and Mary were thinking it would be nice to be there for St Patrick's Day to see the big parade. I said I would be delighted if I could make it for that day, I said it was something I always wanted to see. He said to get everything sorted and as soon as I was ready to give them a call. I got everything ready and got booked up for 8th March 1983, my son Fergal left me to Heathrow. I found it hard to believe that this was for real, I was not worried about flying, I had flown to Ireland lots of times. Our plane taxied out across the airport, they stopped for a while beside the runway, then the pilot came on the tannoy and apologised that they were going to have to return to the terminal as they had recognised a slight smell of fuel coming through the air conditioning. I thought, is my dream not going to come through after all. Anyway we went back to the terminal and had a good meal, we were running a few hours late. It was a big relief when the call was announced for our flight, telling us to get ready to board. After the false start we had a lovely flight after all, we watched movies, we had a lovely dinner, it was all very enjoyable. In no time at all I was eagerly awaiting to see the first glimpse of the U S of A. I was sitting in the seat next to the window, after sometime, I began to see land and houses, I thought, is this it. I asked the man sitting next to me if this was America, he shook his head and laughed, he said, "I'm sorry, but you have a long way to go yet, that's Newfoundland, I said to him that I thought that we would be flying more or less straight across, he explained to me that they had to fly with the curve of the earth. He said, "Just sit back and relax, we'll be there before you know it". When I landed my brother, his wife and family were there to meet me, these were moments to cherish. Arthur took me over to the house the next day to show me all the work that needed doing it, it was a wood structured house, as lot of the houses in the US are. When Arthur showed me around inside the house I realised that there were a lot of places where there was either subsidence or the foundations were collapsing. I could see this was going to be a mighty job, but I had a lot of experience in this kind of work. I had worked for a company called Berry Wiggins many years before, they ran a little Refinery at Grain, their main products were Bitumen and Aquaseal, as far as I know they were the original manufacturers of these products, anyway this is where I learned my trade as a rigger. I was taught by some of the best in the trade, I knew it was going to be a great challenge, but I knew my brother had hands and a great head for working things out, and would treat you as equal to himself, he would always ask your opinion on what you thought was the best way of doing things.

We both knew that the only option was to get some strong jacks and jack up the whole house from the basement, and we would need to get a strong steel plate to put under the jacks, otherwise the weight would break through the concrete floor, and some strong timbers to support the beam which we were jacking up, before we released the jacks. We would only release one jack at any one time, then put the wood packing back in, plus an extra piece of wood to take up the weight, and then do the same with the other jack. You could hardly see how much we gained. After a while Arthur let me get on with it on my own, he had plenty of other work to do, including his day job. I was enjoying it all, it was new lease of life for me. I was using two fifty ton jacks which we hired out a from tool hire place. Arthur went to work the next day and left me to it. I used to feel embarrassed when he would come home in the evening, you could hardly see what I had done in the day, but Arthur understood all the pitfalls of these kind of jobs, so he didn't have to worry. After a few days we could see quite a bit of progress, but that's when I needed to keep an eye on other things, there were there were two apartments in the top section of the house with tenants in both of them. I needed to keep an eye on water and gas lines or sometimes doors would need some alterations, but Arthur would take care of all this when he came home in the afternoon. Eventually we raised the basement six inches. Then we moved into the next floor above us and started the same process again. We had now got the hang of things, as time went by it seemed to get easier.

I really enjoyed what I was doing, but I wanted to get back to be with my two sons again, these were difficult times, there were lots of long drawn out legal documents to be sorted out, I's doted and T's crossed, it takes a long and expensive time. I got back home feeling great, I was relaxed and positive about things. I was only back a few weeks when I managed to get a job back on the Isle of Grain again, but this time on the Grain Power station, which helped me a lot. There could have been a few years work there, but the company decided not to carry out any more new work on No. 5 boiler, so there was going to be redundancies, and as I was one of the last lot to start, I had to go. I managed to get bits of work here and there, then Arthur rang me asking if I could come over again, because he a lot of work that needed doing urgently. Of course I was delighted, I asked him when he wanted me to go, he said as soon as you can or sooner. He said he wanted to get moved in as soon as possible, so I was over there within a few days, and that's the way it was for a number of years, over there for the summer back, here for the winter.

I enjoyed those times very much, I had everything worked out. There was a man whom I knew back home in Ireland, he now lived in Florida, his name was Felix McCarron. He come up to New York for the summer, he had an apartment in New York, and it was cooler there in summer than it would be in Florida. He had taken early retirement, so he had plenty of time to himself, we were good friends back in Ireland, and he played the accordion along with the rest of us in the marching band. We had lots of fun in those days, anyway his sister who still lived Ireland, called him to tell him, that I was in New York staying with my brother Arthur, and it would nice to call and see me. Sure enough he did call to see me, we had a great chat. I said I was thinking about going down to Florida, he asked me when I was thinking of going, I said I was thinking about the end of October. He said that was about the time that he would he would be going back down, and that he would be delighted to give me a lift down there, and that I could stay in his apartment as long as I wanted to. He said it would normally take him about three days to get down there, but he said he was in no hurry, and that we could cross over into different states and see a bit more of the US. So that's what we did and we had a wonderful time, we finally reached Florida, and the good times got better, the weather was lovely and hot, we would go for a swim every morning around seven thirty, then go back to the apartment and have some breakfast and then laze about in the shade for a while. We would go around to different places to see people who had moved to Florida when they retired, I enjoyed every minute of it, Felix had lived life to the full himself, he had some great stories to tell, he was a great friend to have, and sadly he died a few years ago.

For quite some time I had been thinking about applying for a green card, so as I could stay and work in the USA. I went to the US Embassy and got the information that I needed. In order to apply for a green card, they gave me a lot forms that I had to fill in, I needed someone who would be responsible for the first two years that I was in the states, I had my brother Arthur which they accepted. After some time they gave me a card, this was not a green card, it was a card which I could enter the US for limited length of time. I had to take a medical test which I passed, and I went to and fro to the US, which I needed to do just to comply with their regulations. Then I began to think, "should I be doing this", my two boys were still at school and my matrimonial problems were not sorted, so I began to have second thoughts, and I decided to remain in England.

It was the right decision, and thank God everything turned out alright in the end. It was a delicate situation, there was a lot of issues surrounding the divorce to be sorted out, and these things take a long time. I had to tread very carefully not to upset the situation, but after a long spell of negotiations we reached a settlement. Life did not settle down as work was very scarce and I had to find a day's work here and there. I signed on the dole for the first time in my life in 1986 but I never drew any dole money, the jobs they offered me were too far away and having no transport it would have cost me more than I would get on the dole so I choose to work now and then. Arthur still occasionally needed help in America so I would go out to help him and that got me through another few months, and as I said it was mostly in the summer time, it all helped me survive. At this time I only had a small pension from BP, as I could not get their full pension until I reached retirement age, but it did help me a lot. I also played a bit of music at a little club that had opened in the early eighties in Gillingham, St Mary's Social club, this earned me a few pounds here and there. I did not think I was doing anything wrong, I could have sat at home and drew a few pounds from the state and be miserable. I guess that I was lucky I knew a lot of people, and lot of people knew me, either through connections or through the music. I had a lot of Irish connections, over the years I played music in clubs, at weddings, christenings quite regularly, with Billy Carroll, Mick Daly, and another fellow Christy O'Brien.

Music has always been a big part of my life and the regular Monday night sessions that I became a part of with wee Harry at St Marys, have helped me to keep active and involved. To see my 2 sons Liam and Fergal playing music there has made me proud, I like to think that their musical ability is a result of the Sherry genes, or the love of music that I have somehow instilled in them.

I met a lovely girl in 1993 and her name is Helen, and we are still together after 18 years, and those years have been some of the happiest years. I have 2 sons to be proud of, Fergal is a nurse, and Liam has his own business making dental works, I have a fantastic Grandson Ciaron, who has grown into one of the most wonderful men that any man would be proud to call his grandson.

Cassie used to say that I was a natural survivor, I have come through a lot of difficulties, and when I look back I have no regrets, or as the "chairman of the board" said, "regrets, I've had a few, but then again too few to mention",

I have had a lot of happy years . . . .